stress

from burnout to balance

vinay joshi

Response Books
A division of Sage Publications
New Delhi/Thousand Oaks/London

First published in 2005 by

Response Books
A division of Sage Publications India Pvt Ltd
B-42, Panchsheel Enclave
New Delhi 110 017

Sage Publications Inc	**Sage Publications Ltd**
2455 Teller Road	1 Oliver's Yard, 55 City Road
Thousand Oaks, California 91320	London EC1Y 1SP

Published by Tejeshwar Singh for Response Books, typeset in 11.5/14 AGaramond by S.R. Enterprises, New Delhi, and printed at Chaman Enterprises, New Delhi.

Library of Congress Cataloging-in-Publication Data

Joshi, Vinay V., 1963–
    Stress: from burnout to balance/Vinay Joshi.
        p. cm.
    Includes index.
    1. Stress (Psychology) 2. Stress (Physiology) 3. Stress management. I. Title.
    RC455.4.S87J67   616.9'8—dc22   2005   2004022485

ISBN: 0–7619–3312–3 (Pb)   81–7829–466–4 (India–Pb)

Sage Production Team: Leela Kirloskar, Gargi Dasgupta, R.A.M. Brown, Neeru Handa and Santosh Rawat

Contents

List of Figures

List of Appendices

Preface

In routine conversation and publications of general interest, the term stress is usually referred to in the negative sense of 'distress'. In this book, starting with the definition of stress, we examine the way in which our body responds to it. We look at what changes take place in our body in response to stress and how we cope with it. Then, in several subsequent chapters, we examine how the major systems of our body function and see how they are affected by stress. We then come to the very important topic of the psychological factors that affect the stress response. We discuss the scientific experiments that form the foundation of our understanding of psychological factors in the body's response to stress. Recognizing that it is not always possible to eliminate the stressors in our life, we then look at how we can best cope with them. We build on the latest scientific information to see how various things like our psychological makeup, temperament, interaction with society at large and personal beliefs determine the extent to which we are affected by stress. This background then allows us to devise different stress management strategies and choose the best options to lead a healthy life.

The book is intended for people who like to understand the reasoning behind various treatments and suggestions. Many publications give a variety of stress management techniques without explaining why they work. This book covers all aspects of stress, its effects and the various techniques for stress management. Special emphasis has been laid on giving clear explanations of the various problems caused by stress and how the different techniques help alleviate them. Professionals from different fields will find the organization logical and easy to understand.

Vinay Joshi

Acknowledgements

It gives me great pleasure to acknowledge the help of many friends and colleagues in completing this book. I am indebted to all those who took the time out of their busy schedules, to read, comment and suggest changes that needed to be made. I dread to think what form the book would have taken had it not been for their help. Needless to add, any errors and omissions still present are entirely mine.

I am grateful to my dear friend Dr Shreerang Godbole. He reviewed the early manuscript and made valuable suggestions. He is a top-notch endocrinologist with a very busy schedule. Yet, he took the time off to prepare a detailed note pointing out the errors in the book as well as questioning me on some of the facts and claims made. These discussions helped me to revise several chapters and do additional research to understand the subtleties involved. Ravindra (Ravi) Chitnis reviewed one of the early drafts. I would particularly like to mention that in the short period we worked together, I have come to admire his optimism, enthusiasm and positive outlook while analyzing any problem. In the stage when the book existed only as notes, Nitin and Sharmila Paranjpe reviewed the material and gave positive feedback. In particular, a detailed discussion with Nitin acted as an impetus to the writing of this book. Later, Sharmila reviewed the entire manuscript and brought to my notice instances where the explanation required greater clarity. In his position as a CFO, my friend Niteen Gadgil spends all his time looking at endless numbers and figures. However, he showed a great interest in the book and with his customary thoroughness, gave detailed suggestions for improvements. My special thanks to Dr Arvind Godbole, who, with his usual attention to detail, suggested many changes relating to medical facts as well as the structure and organization of the book. As an author with many books to his credit, his suggestions were particularly useful.

My special thanks to my parents, Sulabha and Vasant Joshi, who have stood solidly behind me in all my ventures and activities. Their unquestioned faith in me and unstinted support has been one of the foundations in all my work. My father suggested many changes and helped me to bring focus to the material covered.

At those odd moments of solitude lying awake in bed at three in the morning, I asked myself many times whether writing the book was worth the sacrifice of family time. In this regard, I have to make a special mention of my young son Milind, who had to give up his plans for playing with me or reading together, as I was busy working on the book. Showing maturity beyond his years, he left me alone when I was working in the evenings and over the weekends. With his usual cheery disposition, he accepted my explanations and put away his toys and plans for a later date. Finally, I will only say 'thanks for believing in me', to my best friend, partner and wife, Neelima.

The editorial team at Response Books, Sage Publications, and, in particular, Leela Kirloskar, has been very supportive and offered all help in making this book a reality. I really appreciated Leela's promptness in responding to my queries and found her feedback on the mark. She helped me to bring focus to the material and eliminate the sections that would have distracted the readers.

Chapter 1 | Prologue

*I*t was a moonless night with a light breeze blowing from the south. Walking alone in the dark she could see and hear the others go about their routine activities. She was not really listening but was occasionally startled by the loud noises in the distance. Suddenly, she tensed. She felt rather than saw the danger signals. Her ears pricked up and she became sensitive to the sights and sounds around her. Turning in every direction, she tried to pinpoint the source of her unease—maybe it was the rustle of a body or the silent footstep; she could not be sure. The next moment, all hell broke loose as she saw him right in front of her. The massive figure loomed and bounded straight at her. The stark sight awoke her primordial instinct for survival honed over millions of years through the process of evolution that had built her superb response mechanism. Her heart started pounding, thigh muscles quivered and nostrils flared; with no time to think, she ran for her life. Her pursuer was not so easily put off and, putting on an extra burst of energy, he managed to get within striking distance. She could feel his hot breath and the next moment she felt as if a strong claw had ripped her back. She was dimly aware of the pain and the injury but continued with her flight. Dodging and weaving, she escaped to a nearby area. Her sharpened senses *told her that she was in a familiar area. She could picture a nook, just behind those massive trees where she could hide. Her pursuer was nowhere to be seen and she stood there panting. As she regained her breath, she felt the agonizing pain from her wounds and, for the first time, she realized the extent of her injuries. She was really lucky to have escaped—it could have been much worse! The deer whipped her tail in relief as she tried to regain her breath!*

This is the drama that unfolds practically every night in the savannah or in the jungles, as a tiger, cheetah or some other predator chases a smaller animal. How does the prey respond to the threat of the carnivore intent on killing it? It is remarkable, that within seconds of sensing danger, its heart starts pumping vigorously, muscles get ready for action, and the adrenaline starts flowing. Senses sharpen and the pain is almost forgotten.

Luckily, we humans do not spend our days and nights fleeing from predators or wrestling down our dinner! Most of the diseases that afflicted our ancestors are no longer fatal. We are fortunate to live in an age of tremendous medical advances. As a result, our diseases and causes of death are far different from those which dogged our ancestors. The biggest difference is that the dangers we face are not physical but psychological in nature. It seems that evolution (the process of natural selection) has not kept pace with these advances and our body's response in the face of stress (whether psychological or physical) is the same. The opening paragraph of this chapter described the flight of an animal facing a predator. The body's responses are superbly adapted to deal with such a situation. It should be obvious that activating these same responses when there is no physical danger is not a good idea. This book explores the effects of psychological stress, our body's maladapted stress response and its consequences. Finally, we look at some ways to reduce the effects of stress and to improve our health.

Chapter 2	What is Stress?

Open the papers, watch the news on TV or read any general interest magazine and you will find some discussion on the 'tensions' or 'stress' that we face in this fast-paced computer age. Pseudo-science masquerading as solid scientific research is used to sell merchandise to relieve stress. From 'yogurt' to 'yoga' all are touted as magic remedies to rid the body of toxins generated due to stress. The only thing that seems to work here is the money machine for the sellers! In this chapter, we will try to clear the air about what exactly constitutes stress, why it is bad and what it actually leads to. Details regarding the effects of stress are covered in subsequent chapters and the last two chapters will state some of the scientific techniques for stress management.

As we look around us, we find that most people from the middle class live fairly long and die due to heart diseases, complications from diabetes or conditions related to old age. Most of these diseases are the result of a slow accumulation of damages. For a diabetic or a person suffering from artery blockage, one extra helping of dessert or that additional morsel of fried food is not immediately fatal. The ill effects occur gradually and take many years to manifest. Compare the current scenario with the conditions prevailing about a 100 years ago, when it was common for people to succumb to the bubonic plague, dengue fever, malaria or some other virulent infectious disease. Cholera and typhoid proved to be fatal in many cases. Along with this relatively recent shift in the patterns of diseases, there have been changes in the way we perceive the disease process itself. We have come to recognize the vastly complex intertwining of our biology and emotions, the endless ways in which our personalities, feelings and thoughts both reflect and influence the events in our bodies. A critical recognition of this interaction is the understanding that modern diseases are exacerbated by extreme emotional disturbances. Put in common parlance, 'stress makes us sick'. A critical shift in medicine has been this acceptance of the view that stress plays a significant role in causing or exacerbating the modern diseases of slow accumulation.

The recognition of this connection between emotions and biology is not recent. Reading through the literature on the subject, one can see that many sensitive clinicians intuitively recognized the role of individual differences in the vulnerability to disease. Since the 1940s, the application of rigorous scientific methods to test these vague clinical perceptions has made stress physiology—the study of how the body responds to stressful events—a real discipline. Today, there is an extraordinary amount of physiological, biochemical, and molecular information available on how all sorts of intangibles in our lives—emotional turmoil, psychological characteristics, our place in society, and the sort of society in which we live—can affect very real body events. Purely physical events such as the damage caused due to the gumming up of our arteries by cholesterol, or heart attacks, strokes, diabetes, ulcers, growth in children, pain and a large number of other events are directly influenced by psychological events.

Looking at the evolution of humans and other species, we can see that our ancestors faced serious physical injury, predators and starvation. For an animal like the deer described in the prologue, the most upsetting things in life are *acute physical stressors*. The chase in the savannah is an extremely stressful event and demands immediate physiological adaptations if the prey has to survive. The body's stress response mechanism is brilliantly adapted to handle this sort of emergency.

Chronic physical stressors can also affect an organism. Drought, famine, parasites and other events that cause starvation and other unpleasant complications are central events in the lives of animals and were also experienced by early human ancestors. The body's stress responses are reasonably good at handling these sustained disasters.

Critical to our analysis is a third category of ways to get upset—psychological and social stressors.

Regardless of how poorly we get on with our family members or co-workers, or how incensed we may be with events in our life, we rarely settle these things with physical altercations. Likewise, it is rare for us to stalk and wrestle down our dinner. Essentially, we humans live long enough, well enough and are smart enough to generate all sorts of stressful events purely in our heads. How many elephants worry about their provident fund or what they are going to say in a job interview? A critical point to note, viewed from the perspective of evolution of the animal kingdom, psychological stress is a recent invention. We can experience wildly strong emotions (provoking our bodies into a wild uproar) linked to mere thoughts.

The most important point to note is this—if you are an animal running for your life or sprinting for your meal, your body's physiological response mechanisms are superbly adapted to deal with such short-term emergencies. When we sit around and worry about stressful things, we turn on the same physiological responses—which are potentially a disaster. A large body of scientific literature makes the point that stress-related diseases emerge from the fact that we often activate a physiological system that has evolved to respond to acute physical emergencies, and we turn it on for months on end. What should have been over in a few minutes drags on for months or years and it is obvious that this will lead to major problems.

2.1 Definition of Stress

We will consider a little background information to give some rigour to the term we have been using—*stress*. Living organisms have regular patterns and routines that involve obtaining food breeding, migrating, molting, and hibernating. The acquisition, utilization, and storage of energy reserves (and other resources) are critical to lifetime reproductive success. There are also responses to predictable changes, e.g., seasonal, and unpredictable challenges like storms and natural disasters. Social organization in many populations provides advantages through cooperation in providing basic necessities and beneficial social support. But there are disadvantages owing to conflict in social hierarchies and competition for resources. Here, we discuss the concept of allostasis (maintaining stability through change), as a fundamental process through which organisms actively adjust to both predictable and unpredictable events. One of the central concepts in biology is the notion of a 'balance' where all systems in the body are maintained at a certain optimum level. The scientific term is 'homeostasis' and it is defined as the stability of physiological systems that maintain life. Typically, it applies to a limited number of systems such as acidity, body temperature, glucose levels, and oxygen tension that are truly essential for life and are, therefore, maintained within an optimal range.

This concept has been expanded in recent years to consider a number of changes that take place in our body in response to different events. The scientific term used is 'allostasis' which can be defined simply as achieving stability through change. This is a process that supports homeostasis, i.e., those physiological parameters essential for life as environment change or the person grows through different stages in life (for example, a stage change occurs after childbirth). This means that the 'set points' and other boundaries of control must also change. The body has a number of tools to achieve allostasis which also helps us to clarify an inherent ambiguity in the term 'homeostasis' and distinguishes between the systems that are essential for life (homeostasis) and those that maintain these systems in balance (allostasis) as the environment and life stages change. A number of changes occur in the body to retain allostasis and the primary actors (mediators) in this process are the hormones released by the hypothalamus and the pituitary gland (more of this in the following sections). The allostatic state refers to altered and sustained activity levels of the primary actors that integrate physiology and associated behaviours in response to changing environments and challenges such as social interactions, weather, disease, predators and pollution. An allostatic state results in an imbalance of the primary mediators, reflecting excessive production of some and inadequate production of others. Examples are hypertension, a perturbed rhythm during a period of major depression or after chronic sleep deprivation, chronic elevation of inflammatory cytokines, low cortisol in chronic fatigue syndrome, and imbalance of corticotropin releasing factor (CRF), and cytokines that increase risk for autoimmune and inflammatory disorders.

Some Examples of Allostasis

Consider the normal variations in blood pressure as an example: in the morning, blood pressure rises when we get out of bed and blood flow is maintained to the brain when we stand up in order to keep us conscious. This type of allostasis helps maintain oxygen tension in the brain. There are other examples: Catecholamine and glucocorticoid (stress-response hormone) elevations during physical activity mobilize and replenish, respectively, energy stores needed for brain and body function under challenge. These adaptations maintain essential metabolism and body temperature. Examples in other contexts include changes in food intake and metabolism that females undergo when lactating, or dramatic shifts of metabolism, muscle morphology, and complex patterns of behaviour in migrating birds. These are clearly adjustments to demands dictated by the stages of life, environmental conditions, and social context. Allostatic processes can also go beyond immediate homeostasis, and maintenance of body temperature and dP, to broader aspects of individual survival, e.g., from pathogens or physical danger. For the immune system, acute stress-induced release of catecholamine and glucocorticoid facilitate the movement of immune cells to parts of the body where they are needed to fight an infection or to produce other immune responses. Finally, in the brain, glucocorticoids and catecholamines act in concert to promote the formation of memories of events or potentially dangerous situations so that the individual can avoid them in the future.

What Do We Mean by 'Stress'?

Stress is often defined as a threat, real or implied, to homeostasis. In common usage, stress usually refers to an event or succession of events that cause a response, often in the form of 'distress' but also, in some cases, referring to a challenge that leads to a feeling of exhilaration, as in 'good' stress. But the term 'stress' is full of ambiguities. It is often used to mean the event (stressor) or, sometimes, the response (stress response). Furthermore, it is frequently used in the negative sense of 'distress', and sometimes it is used to describe a chronic state of imbalance. Here *stress will be used to describe events that are threatening to an individual and which elicit physiological and behavioural responses as part of allostasis.*

The response to stress can now be included in the process of allostasis.

The most commonly studied physiological systems that respond to stress are the pituitary secretions and the autonomic nervous system, particularly the sympathetic response of the adrenal gland and the sympathetic nerves. These systems respond in daily life to stressful events as well as to the normal cycle of rest and activity, even though they are frequently identified as 'stress response systems'. Behaviourally, the responses to stress may consist of 'fight or flight' reactions or, in humans, involve health-related behaviours such as excessive eating, alcohol consumption, smoking, and other forms of substance abuse. Reaction to a potentially stressful situation could also be an increased state of vigilance, enhanced by anxiety and worrying particularly when the threat is ill-defined or imaginary and when there is no clear alternative behavioural response that would end the threat. Behavioural responses to stress and these states of anxiety are capable of exacerbating existing conditions.

Protection vs Damage

From the standpoint of survival and health of the individual, the most important feature of mediators associated with allostasis is that they have protective effects in the short run. However, they can have damaging effects in the long run if there are many adverse life events or if hormone secretion is poorly regulated as in a sustained allostatic state that leads to allostatic overload. We shall now illustrate how the immediate effects of the secretion of mediators of allostasis such as glucocorticoids and catecholamines are largely protective and adaptive. We then note the damaging consequences that result from overproduction and/or dysregulation of the same mediators. Glucocorticoids, so named because of their ability to promote conversion of protein and fats into usable carbohydrates, serve the body well in the short run by replenishing energy reserves after a period of activity such as running away from a predator. Glucocorticoids also act on the brain to increase appetite for food and to increase activity and food seeking behaviour, thus regulating behaviours that control energy intake and expenditure. This is very useful when we have to run several miles, but it is not beneficial when we grab a bag of potato chips while sitting at our desk and working on a computer. Inactivity and lack of energy expenditure creates a situation where chronically elevated glucocorticoids can impede the action of insulin to promote glucose uptake. One of the results of this interaction is that insulin levels increase. High insulin and glucocorticoid concentrations promote the deposition of body fat. This combination of hormones also promotes formation of plaques in coronary arteries.

Free living animals responding to storms, change in social status, or human disturbance that result in reduced access to resources such as food and shelter increase glucocorticoid secretion to facilitate foraging and promote gluconeogenesis (generating glucose in the liver). There is also an inhibition of processes not essential for survival (e.g., reproduction), an increase in activity associated with moving away from the perturbation or finding shelter, and promotion of night restfulness with a saving in energy. Glucocorticoids act in concert with chemicals in the central nervous system, to orchestrate these complex physiological and behavioural responses to perturbations of the environment. For the heart, we see a similar paradoxical role of allostasis mediators. Our blood pressure rises and falls during the day as physical and emotional demands change, providing adequate blood flow as needed. Yet, repeatedly elevated blood pressure resulting from additional allostatic load promotes generation of atherosclerotic plaque, particularly when combined with a supply of cholesterol, lipids, and oxygen-free radicals that damage the coronary artery walls. Beta-blockers[1] are known to inhibit this cascade of events and to slow down the arteriosclerosis. Thus, despite their short-term adaptive roles, catecholamines and the combination of glucocorticoids and insulin can have dangerous effects on the body.

The nervous system interprets which events are 'stressful' and determines behavioural and physiological responses to the stressor, and it shows a similar paradoxical action of the mediators of allostatic load. In the brain, strong emotions frequently lead to 'flashbulb' memories, e.g., where we were and what we were doing when we heard of Indira Gandhi's assassination, the horrible events of 11 September 2001, or remembering the location and events associated with a very positive life event like proposing marriage or receiving a promotion or award. Both catecholamine receptors and

---

[1] These blood pressure lowering drugs are commonly called beta-blockers though the correct scientific term is beta-adrenergic receptor blockers.

glucocorticoids play an important role in establishing these long lasting memories. A number of brain structures participate along with the autonomic nervous system. A section of the brain called the amygdala plays an important role in this type of memory. It is aided by the autonomic nervous system, which picks up a signal from circulating epinephrine, and by the hippocampus, which helps us remember 'where we were and what we were doing' at the time the amygdala was turned on in such a powerful way. Thus, epinephrine and glucocorticoids promote the memory of events and situations, which in future may be dangerous. This is an adaptive and beneficial function.

The paradox for the brain comes when there is repeated stress over many days or when allostatic load forces gluco-corticoid levels to remain high. Then there is atrophy of brain cells and inhibition of ongoing regeneration of nerve cells. After very prolonged periods of allostatic load, allostatic over-load may occur and neurons may actually die. Through some or all of these processes, the hippocampus (a portion of the brain) undergoes a shrinkage in size, with impairment of de-clarative, contextual, and spatial memory. This can be picked up in the human brain by neuropsychological testing accom-panied by Magnetic Resonance Imaging (MRI) in such con-ditions as recurrent depressive illness, Cushing's syndrome, post-traumatic stress disorder, mild cognitive impairment in aging, and schizophrenia.

2.2 Selye and His Ulcerated Rats

The generality of the stress response (it is the same for a variety of stressors) was first appreciated about 70 years back by one of the pioneers of the field of stress physiology (Hans Selye). It can be said that the field was born because Selye was a very insightful scientist but very clumsy at handling laboratory rats. His fascinating story starts in the 1930s when he was just beginning his work on endocrinology (study of hormones). As a young assistant professor he was looking for a promising area of research. As luck would have it, a biochemist down the hall had just isolated some sort of extract from the ovary and everybody was wondering what the extract did to the body. So, Selye obtained some of the stuff from the biochemist and set about his experiments. He attempted to inject his study rats daily but was very clumsy. He would drop them, chase them all over the laboratory and flail at them till he finally caught up with them.

Several months later, Selye examined the rats and discovered that they had peptic ulcers, greatly enlarged adrenal glands and shrunken immune tissues. Selye was delighted and thought that he had discovered the effects of the mysterious ovarian extract. Being a good scientist, he repeated his experiment with two groups of rats. One group received the extract and other received saline solution alone. His handling of the rats had not improved and all rats were dropped, chased, dropped and caught while receiving their injections. At the end of the experiment, both groups exhibited the same symptoms—ulcers, enlarged adrenals and shrunken immune tissue. Faced with such a situation, the average scientist would have quietly burned his notes and slunk off to more promising fields like law or tried to get an MBA degree! Selye instead reasoned through what he had observed. The extract could not cause the effects and the only thing common to both groups were the trauma-filled injections. He reasoned that the changes were the body's response to generic unpleasantness. To test this idea, he put some rats on the top of the terrace in winter and some near the boiler in summer. In all cases, he found the same incidence of ulcer, and atrophy of the immune tissues.

We now know that Selye had observed the tip of the iceberg of stress-related disease. Legend has it (reading the literature it seems that this legend was mostly promulgated by Selye himself) that it was Selye who borrowed the term stress from the field of engineering*. Selye was the first to theorize that—

- The body has a surprisingly similar set of responses to a broad array of stressors.
- Under certain conditions, stressors will make you sick.

In an interesting postscript to this story, Selye wrestled with the puzzle of why stress response makes us sick and came up with an answer. Unfortunately, his answer was sufficiently wrong that it is generally supposed to have cost him the Nobel Prize!

With the knowledge available now, it is pretty easy to see how turning on the stress response in the face of psychological stress can make us sick. The things that our body does in response to stress are generally shortsighted and inefficient.

---

* Other researchers had used this term a decade earlier.

They are the sort of costly things the body has to do to respond effectively in an emergency. If every day living becomes an emergency, you will eventually have to pay the price. If you constantly mobilize energy at the cost of its storage, you will never manage to have a surplus. You will fatigue more rapidly and run a high risk of developing diabetes. The consequences of chronically overactivating your cardiovascular system are similarly damaging. Raising your blood pressure to 180/120 when sprinting for your life is being superbly adaptive but the same blood pressure in response to the mess in your children's room will lead to disaster. In children, chronic stress can lead to a disorder called 'stress dwarfism'. In females, chronic stress can lead to irregular menstrual cycles and, in males, sperm counts and testosterone levels may decline. In both sexes, interest in sexual behaviour will decline and the immune system will be suppressed. But that is only the start of the problems—suppressing immune functions for too long can lead to other horrendous diseases (the tragedy of AIDS has taught us that lesson very well). Finally, the same systems of the brain that function so well during stress can be damaged by a class of hormones released during the stress response and can lead to neurological conditions like depression.

2.3 A Representation of Stress Response

All of this is pretty grim news. In the face of repeated stressors, we may be able to precariously retain the state of allostasis, but it does not come cheap and the efforts to re-establish the balance will eventually wear us down.

An interesting model/analogy used in stress literature is that of 'two elephants on a seesaw'. Here is a way to think about it: put two small children on a seesaw and they can pretty readily balance themselves on it. This represents that state of the body in allostasis when nothing stressful is going on and the children represent the low levels of stress hormones in the body. In contrast, the torrents of hormones in response to severe stress can be thought of as two massive elephants on the seesaw. Sure, they can balance but with great difficulty. Repeatedly getting the two elephants to balance can lead to problems—

- First, enormous potential energy is required to maintain the balance. That energy is wasted instead of being put to more useful tasks like growth in the body. This is equivalent to diverting funds from long-term projects for short-term emergency management. Obviously, a wasteful way to manage your finances.
- Extending our analogy further, the mere presence of two elephants is damaging. The elephants trample over everything in their way; they leave a lot of mess behind them and by their sheer weight wear out the seesaw. This is a crucial point—it is hard to fix one major problem in the body without knocking something else out of balance. You may be able to solve one problem using the elephants (massive stress hormones) but you will certainly damage some other area.
- A final subtle point, once the two elephants are balanced on the seesaw it is very difficult for them to get off. Either one jumps off and the other comes crashing down

or their actions are coordinated which is an extremely delicate task. This reveals that stress-related diseases can arise from turning off the stress responses too slowly, or turning off different components at different speeds.

Another way to look at it is to visualize two tug-of-war teams skillfully supporting their rope with a minimum of tension; the body works to carefully maintain metabolic equilibrium by making adjustments whenever something disturbs this balance. The strong men in these teams are hormones. The trouble is that some stress-response hormones don't know when to quit pulling. They remain active in the brain for too long and end up causing problems all around.

The punch line of the preceding discussion on stress response is that if you repeatedly turn on the stress response or cannot turn it off at the end of the stressful event, the response can become as damaging as some stressors themselves. A large percentage of what we think of when we talk of stress-related diseases are disorders of excessive stress response. It is actually more accurate to say that chronic stressors can potentially cause diseases that will make you sick. If you already have such a disease, stress increases the risk of your defenses being overwhelmed by the disease. This may sound like nitpicking but is very important from the point of designing ways to intervene and prevent stress-related diseases. Think about it for a moment: The more steps that we put between the stressor and the disease, the more are the places for intervention and prevention of damage.

Chapter 3 | Stress Response

We begin our study of the body's response to stress from the very top—the brain. Intuitively, we all understand that our brain controls the functions of our body. We know that we can think of moving an arm or a leg and it happens. In this chapter, we will take a look at how the brain actually exerts control and which systems are activated or suppressed as we undergo stress. In subsequent chapters, we will see what the effects of these stress-induced actions are and how they can make us sick.

3.1 Autonomic Nervous System

The principal way in which the brain communicates with the rest of the body is through neural telephone lines (like the land-line telephones). The body also uses the mobile phone service—the use of hormones[1] in the blood to send messages to distant parts of the body. The 'land telephone' system consists of nerves that start from the brain, go down the spinal cord and branch out to the periphery of the body. One part of this system is simple and we all understand it—

---

[1] The word hormone comes from a Greek word meaning to 'set in motion'.

the voluntary system. As the name implies this is the system we use to move our arms or legs when we want to. The other half of the system is called the autonomic system. Again, as the name suggests, things here happen automatically and we do not have much control over them. This system controls things like our digestion, heartbeats, sweat glands and so on. It is the autonomic system that is of interest to us as it is involved directly in the body's response to stress. The autonomic system also consists of two parts—the sympathetic and the parasympathetic systems.

Originating in the brain, sympathetic nerve projections exit the spine and branch out to nearly every organ and blood vessel. These nerves are so pervasive that they are even attached to the tiny muscles attached to the hair on our body.[2] This system is activated in response to any stress. It helps mediate vigilance, arousal, activation and mobilization. A feeble joke can be used to describe the action as mediating behaviour such as flight, fright and fight. This system is turned on when things get too exciting or too alarming, as is the case during stress.

How does the nervous system go about controlling the different organs? The nerve endings of the sympathetic system release epinephrine and closely related substance norepinephrine (the other names in use are adrenaline and noradrenaline). The actual secretion of epinephrine is from the sympathetic nerve endings in the adrenal glands. Norepinephrine is secreted

---

[2] When activated they make the hair on our arms stand up and also cause goose bumps in areas where there is no hair.

by all the other sympathetic nerve endings throughout the body. Within seconds of the body being stressed, these chemical messengers are secreted and they in turn kick the various organs into action.

The parasympathetic nervous system plays the opposite role. It mediates calm and vegetative activities. It promotes growth, energy storage and other optimistic activities. Everything but the four Fs is controlled by the sympathetic nervous system. Thus, the two parts of the autonomic nervous system work in opposition. The projections from both these parts into an organ when activated bring out opposite results. Therefore, it would be a disaster if both systems were to be activated at the same time. Naturally, our body has a number of mechanisms to ensure that the two systems are not activated simultaneously. In particular, the part of the brain that activates the sympathetic component during a stressful period also inhibits the parasympathetic system.

3.2 The Hormonal System

Continuing with our telephone analogy for brain communication, the body uses both land-based telephones (nerves from the brain to all organs of the body) as well as mobile telephony. The mobile telephones are represented by the hormonal system. We saw that chemical messengers from the sympathetic nerve endings direct the organs to respond to stressful events. If the same chemicals are released into the blood and affect events far and wide, they are called hormones. The hormones are transported in the common medium (blood) just like the mobile telephone messages travel through the air. There are a number of glands in the body that secrete hormones. Extending our analogy further, it is clear that the message will be understood only by the telephone system for which it is intended. In our daily usage, there are multiple mobile phone companies and each requires a special card that must be put in our phone before we can make and receive calls. Similarly, there are multiple hormones but the organs respond to the hormones for which they have the correct 'phone-card'—receptor (to give it the correct scientific name). Most hormones circulate in the blood and essentially come into contact with all the cells. Only those cells with the receptors for that hormone will react to the hormonal message. These cells, not surprisingly are called target cells for the hormone. Hormone receptors are found either exposed on the surface of the cell or within the cell, depending on the type of hormone.

In very basic terms, the binding of a hormone to a receptor triggers a cascade of reactions within the cell that affects its function. So, what is the purpose of introducing all this information on hormone receptors and target cells? It will help us to understand one of the key control mechanisms as well as the cause of diseases which will be discussed in the following chapters.

The receptor mechanism allows the body to control the effects of certain hormones. Metaphorically, say, the cells take a dislike to some hormone like insulin because it keeps pestering them all the time. They decide they have had enough bossing from insulin and they simply reduce the number of receptors for insulin. Neat trick; the cell is no longer as sensitive to the hormone signals as it was before. To give the correct scientific jargon—the cell has downgraded the receptor for that particular hormone. Good for the cell, not so good for the rest of the body. In fact, as we will see in chapter 4, this is pretty much what happens in the case of people who get Type-II diabetes. Just as the cells downgrade the receptors, the sympathetic system downgrades the receptors for particular hormones when it wishes to minimize the hormonal effects.

Depending on the binding, there are two important terms for the molecules that perform the actual binding—

- **Agonists**[3] are molecules that bind to the receptor and induce all the post-receptor events that lead to the desired biological effect. Natural hormones are themselves agonists.
- **Antagonists** are molecules that bind to the receptor and block binding of the agonist, but fail to trigger intracellular signalling events.

Antagonists are like bureaucrats—they do not perform useful work themselves, but block the activities of those that do have the capacity to contribute! Hormone antagonists are widely used as drugs for obvious reasons. Suppose, some hormone is being produced like crazy in the body—all the

---

[3] With my tongue firmly in cheek, I suggest that this is an impressive term to use in casual party chatter! Conveys the impression that you are well versed. Better yet, try to use this term as part of some new management jargon. Come up with a slogan like—the manager is an agonist! Be an agonist! Let your subordinates scramble to decipher your new directive.

fancy control systems seem to have failed. The simple solution is to have a chemical that will act as an antagonist. And hey presto! The effects of the hormone are dramatically reduced! This is like talking on the phone to somebody else all the time so that other phone calls cannot come through. No wonder the hormone cannot get through to the cell as it finds the receiver busy. It does not matter how much hormone is present—the listener has not heard the message.

3.3 Who is the Boss?

An interesting question to ask is: How are these hormone secretions controlled? Actually, the better question to ask is: who controls these glands that secrete the hormones? Till the 1930s, it was widely assumed that there was no master control for these hormonal glands and that somehow the glands 'knew' what they were doing and responded to various events correctly. With time, scientists determined that the different glands were not autonomous but were under the control of something else. It was observed that a gland (called the pituitary) located just below the brain seemed to affect the output of other glands. Like many scientific discoveries this was demonstrated negatively by studying patients with damaged pituitary glands. In such cases, the hormone secretion through the rest of the body became disordered. Careful scientific experiments showed that a peripheral gland releases its hormone only if the pituitary first releases a hormone that tells the gland to do its job. The pituitary contains a whole array of hormones that run the hormonal show in the body. The obvious conclusion was that the pituitary was the real master gland of the body. The popular press[4] at that time, helped to disseminate this view far and wide.

By the 1950s many scientists were discovering that the pituitary was not the real master gland at all. The simplest experiment involved removing the pituitary from an animal and putting it in a bowl filled with pituitary nutritive material. Observations showed that the pituitary behaved abnormally. The sceptics argued that the pituitary was traumatized and taking anything out of the body and putting it in a bowl will mean that it will not secrete a lot of hormones. Interestingly, while levels of some hormones secreted were quite low, the others were secreted at extremely high levels. It turned out that the pituitary was acting erratically because it really was clueless about the hormonal plan and it was not receiving any orders from its boss. The boss turns out to be the brain.

Experiments clearly showed the brain to be in charge of the pituitary. If a portion of the brain near the pituitary is destroyed, the pituitary starts to act erratically. It was clear that the brain must have some mechanism that it uses to communicate with the pituitary. As the pituitary is located so close to the brain, by all logic, there should be nerve projections from the brain to the pituitary (similar to the nerve projections going to the different parts of the body like the heart) and for the brain to release neurotransmitters to communicate with the pituitary. Unfortunately, no one could find these projections. One of the pioneers in this field, the

---

[4] The *Reader's Digest* ran a series of articles on different organs of the body with titles such as 'I am Joe's Kidney', 'I am Joe's pancreas' and so on. The article on the pituitary trotted out the master gland theory.

physiologist Geoffrey Harris proposed that the brain was also a hormonal gland and that it released hormones into the bloodstream like the other glands. These hormones travelled through the bloodstream and reached the pituitary where they directed its actions. A lot of scientists at that time thought that these ideas were outlandish. Two scientists, Roger Guillemin and Andrew Schally, began looking for these brain hormones. What unfolded was a drama worthy of a movie (well, if not a full movie at least a mini-serial on TV)!

3.4 The Race

The task of finding the brain hormones that communicated with the pituitary was stupendously difficult. The circulatory system between the brain and the pituitary is miniscule—smaller than the full stop at the end of this sentence. These hormones, if they existed, would be in such minute quantities that they would not be traceable in the general circulation of the blood. The best bet was to look for the traces of these hormones in the tiny bits of tissue at the base of the brain. This tissue contains the blood vessels that go from the brain to the pituitary.

In the initial phase, Guillemin and Schally collaborated and started their quest for the brain hormones. In the late 1950s, they went their separate ways.[5] They were no doubt

---

[5] The actual reason for their parting seems to be lost in historical obscurity. Perhaps, while working late one evening, they sniped at each other or made rude remarks while passing each other in the corridor. Whatever the reason, they parted ways and a notorious animosity developed between the two men.

drawn to this stupendously difficult problem by the abstract intellectual puzzle, the fame and glory to be had at the end plus their mutual hatred!

The parting of the two scientists could not have been over the direction of their research as both of them essentially followed the same path. The problem they faced could be described as—how do you find a hormone that may or may not exist and even if it does, occurs in such tiny amounts in an extremely small circulatory system, which cannot be accessed? Both scientists used the same strategy. They collected animal brains from slaughterhouses and cut out the small part at the bottom that is near the pituitary. In a blender they combined these brain parts to get a mash and then attempted to purify the mash. The purified droplets were then injected in rats to see if the pattern of pituitary hormones released was altered. If it did, they went on to purify that droplet and make an artificial version of it. A straightforward approach in theory but the effort took them years.

There were several problems that confounded the two scientists. At best, there was a miniscule portion of the hormones in any one brain. To get any reasonable quantity for analysis, they required truckloads of animal brains. Chemists had to design new ways to isolate the different chemicals in the brain. New theories and practices had to be invented for analysis and synthesis of the chemicals. This was not just a mindless task but involved a lot of complicated science. New methods of testing the effects of hormones on animals were invented. The enormously difficult problem was made worse by the fact that a number of people in the scientific community believed that these brain hormones were fictitious and the two scientists were wasting a lot of time and money!

The search for the hormones led to a new corporatization of scientific research. Whole teams of physicians, chemists, physiologists, and biochemists were involved in isolating these putative hormones. Finally, it worked. In a 'short' span of 14 years in 1969, the chemical structure of the first releasing hormone was published. So, asks the breathless reader, who won? Just like the problem, the answer is complicated and I urge the reader to turn to Appendix 1 for the final result! Everyone was very happy and the by-then-deceased Geoffrey Harris was proved correct.

So, the brain turns out to be the master gland after all and like they say in the children's song—*the brain is the boss of the body. It tells everybody what to do....* It is now recognized that the base of the brain, the hypothalamus, contains a huge array of the hormones that instruct the pituitary. In turn, the pituitary releases hormones that control the action of the other glands of the body.

3.5 Control Systems for Hormone Secretion

The effects of the hormones depend largely on their concentration in blood and extracellular fluid. Almost inevitably, disease results when hormone concentrations are either too high or too low, and precise control over circulating concentrations of hormones is, therefore, crucial.

The concentration of hormone as seen by target cells is determined by three obvious factors—the rate of production of the hormone, the rate at which it is delivered, and how long it takes to degrade.

To decide how much hormone should be circulating at any given time, good control systems need to be in place. Feedback circuits are at the root of most control mechanisms in our body, and are particularly prominent in the hormonal (endocrine) system. Instances of positive feedback certainly occur, but negative feedback is much more common, particularly so for the stress hormones. We are familiar with this negative feedback control system from the air conditioners used to cool the rooms in our homes or the water tank in the toilet. In the case of air conditioners, when the temperature rises above a certain set point, cool air is blown into the room. As the room cools down and the temperature drops, a feedback is sent to the thermostat. When the temperature drops below the set point, the thermostat is triggered and the cooling stops. When the temperature rises again, the negative feedback is stopped and the cooling cycle starts.

3.6 Hormones of the Stress Response

The preceding section showed how the brain controls the secretion of various hormones. The interesting point to note is that the brain releases hormones that direct the pituitary to work in two ways—either secrete some hormones or suppress others.

Here, we will look at the various hormones involved in stress response and this section is not for the faint-hearted.

Don't get stressed by the long names. You have been warned in advance! I will try to keep the information to the minimum that is required to get an idea of the hormones involved in stress response. Two hormones that we saw previously, epinephrine and norepinephrine, are released by the sympathetic nervous system. A second important class of hormones is the steroid hormones. The term steroid is a general one used to describe the chemical structure of five classes of hormones:

- Androgens—these are the anabolic steroids[6] like testosterone.
- Estrogens—in the news recently as a controversial treatment for menopause.
- Progestins
- Mineralocorticoids
- Glucocorticoids

The last named, glucocorticoids, are one of the key stress-response hormones and have an action similar to epinephrine. The difference is really in the duration of action. Epinephrine acts instantly and the effects last for a few minutes while glucocorticoids provide the backup and have effects that last for several hours. Glucocorticoids are released

---

[6] The steroids loved by various Olympic athletes to enhance performance, with the nasty side effect that if detected in the blood you get thrown out of the Olympics and lose any medals you may have won!

by the adrenal glands. In times of stress, the brain controls the release of glucocorticoids through a three-step process—

- The hypothalamus secretes an array of releasing hormones into the hypothalamus-pituitary circulatory system. The principal hormone is CRF (Corticotropin Releasing Factor).
- Within 15 to 20 seconds of its release, CRF triggers the pituitary to release the hormone corticotropin (also known as ACTH).
- ACTH travels through the bloodstream and reaches the adrenal glands and within a few minutes the adrenals release glucocorticoids.

Epinephrine and glucocorticoids account for majority of things that happen in the body as a result of stress.

The pituitary also secretes the hormone prolactin, which among other things plays a role in suppressing reproduction during stress. The pituitary and the brain release a class of morphine-like substances called endorphins and enkephalins that help reduce pain perception. The pituitary also releases antidiuretic hormone (vasopressin) that plays a role in the cardiovascular stress response. The pancreas releases a hormone called glucagons which, in conjunction with the glucocorticoids and the sympathetic nervous system, raise the levels of circulating blood glucose.

Just as some of the hormones are released during stress, a number of them are suppressed. The secretion of the various reproductive hormones like estrogen, progesterone and testosterone are suppressed. Growth hormones and insulin secretion are inhibited.

Finally, a comment on the names given to hormones and what some have called the 'tyranny of terminology'. Hormones are inevitably named shortly after their discovery, when understanding is necessarily rudimentary. They are often named for the first physiological effect observed or for their major site of synthesis. As knowledge and understanding of the hormone grow, the original name often appears inappropriate or too restrictive, but it has become entrenched in literature and is rarely changed. In other situations, a single hormone will be referred to by more than one name. The problem is that the names given to hormones often end up being either confusing or misleading. The solution is to view names as identifiers rather than strict guidelines to source or function.

3.7 Subtleties of the Stress Response

So far, in our discussion, we have emphasized how the body has a fairly generalized stress response to any stressor. A physical danger or a purely psychological stress and the response of the body is pretty much the same. Hidden in this generalization are many subtleties. Obviously, a lot of the technical details are beyond the scope of this book. However, we will look at some of the aspects that will give an idea of the complications.

The first simple point is that not all species respond to stressors in the same way. Though animals are used in the laboratories, humans do not necessarily have the same response.[7]

Another complication has to do with the pattern of stress responses to different stressors. Scientists look at the pattern of release of the hormones for a particular stressor and they term it the 'hormonal signature' of a particular stressor. The basic hormonal system outlined in the previous section holds true for massive physical stressors. Subtle stressors will not have the same hormonal effect—for example, public speaking may be stressful but will obviously not elicit the same stress response as some grave physical danger. Typically, scientists have found that a high degree of sympathetic activity is found in the case of anxiety and vigilance while higher secretions of glucocorticoids mark depression like symptoms. Similarly, epinephrine and norepinephrine are not released in response to all stressors.

We have made the point that the stress response was crafted by millions of years of evolution and is ideal for dealing with life-threatening physical stressors encountered by our ancestors. In that context, it is fair to question the role of glucocorticoids. We mentioned earlier that glucocorticoids back up the action of epinephrine over minutes and hours. So, how many chases in the wild or sprints across the grasslands go on for hours? Typically, such contests are over in five to ten minutes. For example, a cheetah can sprint for only eight or ten minutes before it gives up. Then, of what

---

[7] For example, when stressed, growth hormones decline in rats while they increase in humans transiently.

use is the action of glucocorticoids? This is an important area of research and a number of theories have been proposed. The best explanation so far is that the glucocorticoids are not really a stress response but they help mediate the recovery from the stress response and they help the body prepare for the next stressor. These are tentative theories backed up by some experiments—so stay tuned for more developments in this field.

One final note (the point that gives us a ray of hope for dealing with stressors): Stress response depends on psychological factors and two identical stressors can cause widely different responses depending on the psychological context. It is fascinating that the physical response of our body to a stressor can be controlled by our mind or by the way we perceive things. This is a very powerful concept and we will explore this topic further in the following chapters.

To conclude, I will emphasize the main thesis of this book—in spite of some differences in response to various stressors, the major stress response is pretty consistent for a wide variety of stressors. In subsequent chapters, we will explore the various systems of the body and the effects of stress response on them.

Chapter 4   Metabolism

The basic process of digestion comprises breaking down pieces of animals and vegetables so that they can be transformed into pieces of human body. This may seem facetious but that is the essence of digestion.

Simply put, the digestive system is a portal for nutrients from the environment to gain access to the circulatory system. Before the transfer can occur, foodstuff first has to be reduced to very simple molecules by a combination of mechanical and enzymatic degradation. The resulting sugars, amino acids, fatty acids and the like are then transported across the epithelium lining the intestine into the bloodstream. The focus of this section is to examine the 'big picture' of digestive physiology and to look at fundamental aspects of the digestive system. Consider for a moment a plate of *biryani*. The purpose of eating *biryani*, other than simple hedonism, is to assimilate the nutrients it contains and to make them available to build, repair and maintain your own tissues, as well as provide energy for daily activities.

You may ask yourself what nutrients are present in a *biryani* that the body can assimilate? The body has to provide the means to carefully break them down into much smaller molecules that can be imported into blood. Luckily, your digestive system takes care of this very complex process so efficiently that most of the time you don't even need to think about it.

At its simplest, the digestive system is a tube running from mouth to anus. This tube is like an assembly line, or more accurately, a disassembly line. Its chief goal is to break down huge macromolecules (proteins, fats and starch), which cannot be absorbed intact, into smaller molecules (amino acids, fatty acids and glucose) that can be absorbed through the walls of the tube, and into the circulatory system for dissemination.

The breakdown of food, like *biryani,* is accomplished through a combination of mechanical and enzymatic processes. To accomplish this breakdown, the digestive tube requires considerable assistance from accessory digestive organs such as the salivary glands, liver and pancreas, which dump their secretions into the tube. The name 'accessory' should not be taken to mean dispensable; indeed, without pancreatic enzymes you would find it very difficult to live.

In many ways, the digestive system can be thought of as a well-run factory in which a large number of complex tasks are performed.

Each part of the digestive tube performs at least some of these tasks, and different regions of the tube have unique and important specializations. Like any well-run factory, proper function of the digestive system requires robust control systems. These control systems must facilitate communication among different sections of the digestive tract (i.e., control on the factory floor), and between the digestive tract and the brain (i.e., between workers and management). Control of digestive function is achieved through a combination of electrical and hormonal messages, which originate either within the digestive system's own nervous and endocrine systems, or from the central nervous system and endocrine organs such as the adrenal gland. Different parts of these systems are constantly talking to one another. The basic messages are along the lines of *I've just received an extraordinary load of food; so I suggest you get prepared* (stomach to large intestine) or *For goodness sake, please slow down until I can catch up with what you've already given me* (small intestine to stomach).

The breakdown of complex food matter into its simplest parts—amino acids, glucose, free fatty acids and glycerol—is mainly accomplished in the gastrointestinal tract by enzymes (chemicals that degrade complex molecules). These simple building blocks thus produced are absorbed into the bloodstream for delivery to whichever cell in the body needs them. Once this is done, the cells have the ability to use these building blocks to construct the proteins, fats and carbohydrates needed to stay in business. And just as importantly, the fatty acids and sugars can also be burned by the body to provide energy to do all the construction.

To give a simple analogy—it is rare these days for the wealthy to walk around with all their money in their pockets, or stuff their cash inside their matresses. Instead, surplus wealth is stored elsewhere, in forms more complex than cash—mutual funds, government bonds, and offshore bank accounts! In the same way, surplus energy is not kept in the body's form of cash (amino acids, glucose, fatty acids) but stored in more complex forms. Enzymes in the fat cells can combine fatty acids and glycerol to form triglycerides. Accumulate enough of these in the fat cells and you grow fat. Meanwhile, enzymes in cells throughout the body can cause succession of molecules of glucose to stick together. These long chains, sometimes thousands of glucose molecules, are called glycogen. Most glycogen formation occurs in our muscles and liver. Similarly, the enzymes in cells throughout the body can combine long strings of amino acids and turn them into proteins.

The hormone that stimulates the transport and storage of these building blocks into target cells is insulin. In a sense, insulin plans for our metabolic future. Eat a big lunch and insulin pours out of the pancreas into the bloodstream, stimulating the transport of fatty acid to fat cells, stimulating glycogen and protein synthesis. To continue with our finance analogy, insulin fills out the deposit slips at our fat banks. It turns out that we even secrete insulin when we are about to fill our bloodstream with all those nutritive building blocks. If you eat dinner each day at 8 p.m., by 7:45 p.m. the parasympathetic nervous system is already stimulating insulin secretion in anticipation.

4.1 Energy Mobilization During a Stressor

This strategy of breaking food into its simplest parts and reconverting it into complex forms for storage is precisely what our body should do when we have eaten plenty. And this is precisely what the body should not do in the face of an immediate physical emergency (stressor). First, the body turns down the parasympathetic nervous system and down goes insulin secretion. Second, the body makes sure that energy storage is stopped. With the onset of stress, the body releases glucocorticoids, which block the transport of nutrients into fat cells. This counteracts the effect of any insulin still floating around.

In addition to halting the storage of energy, you want your body to gain access to the energy already stored. You want to dip into your bank account, turn stored nutrients into your body's equivalent of cash to get you through this crisis. Our body reverses all the storage steps, through the release of stress-response hormones. These cause triglycerides to be broken down in the fat cells and, as a result, free fatty acids and glycerol pour into the bloodstream. The same hormones trigger the degradation of glycogen to glucose in cells throughout the body and the glucose is then flushed into the bloodstream. These hormones also cause proteins in non-exercising muscles to be converted back into individual amino acids.

The stored nutrients have now been converted into simpler forms. Our body makes another simplifying move. Amino acids are not a very good source of energy, but glucose is. Our body shunts the amino acids to the liver, where they are converted into glucose. The liver can also generate new glucose; a process called 'gluconeogenesis' and this glucose is now available for energy during the emergency.

As a result of all these processes, a lot of energy is available to the exercising muscles. There is a burst of activity, the emergency is averted and the extra energy is consumed. Say, you are running away from some danger, it does not make sense to provide extra energy to the arm muscles. The stress hormones (glucocorticoids and the rest of the gang) block energy uptake into the non-exercising muscles. Somehow the exercising muscles override this blockade and grab all the nutrients floating around in circulation. No one knows how this signalling takes place.

As will be clear, this response to stress is great in the face of physical stress. Not such a great idea when the stress is purely psychological—uncomfortable social settings, public speaking, or fights (verbal) with your wife. All the free energy floating in the blood and no muscles to use it!

4.2 So Why Do We Get Sick?

If mobilization of energy in response to stress works so wonderfully, why should it make us sick in face of chronic psychological stress? For many of the same reasons that constantly running to the bank and drawing cash from the savings accounts is a foolish way to handle your money.

At the most basic level, it is inefficient. Every time we store energy away from circulation and then return it, we lose a fair chunk of potential energy. In effect, you are penalized if you activate the stress response too often. You wind up expending so much energy that you tire more readily. Finally, with enough stress, you begin to have problems with one type of diabetes called Type II diabetes. This takes some explaining.

4.3 Diabetes

There are two types of diabetes—the first is Type I or juvenile or insulin-dependent diabetes. For reasons that are still not clear, the immune system decides that cells in the pancreas which secrete insulin are, in fact, foreign invaders and attacks them. This leaves a person with very little insulin and, therefore, little availability to promote the uptake of glucose (and indirectly fatty acids) into target cells. Big trouble—the cells are starving! In addition, there is all that glucose and fatty acid circulating in the bloodstream—like gangsters with no place to go and they show their hand—blood vessels in kidneys gum up, arteries get atherosclerotic plaque and make it impossible for oxygen and glucose to be delivered to the tissues causing little strokes and chronic pain. They also link proteins together in the eyes to form cataracts. Bad news all around.

If you have insulin-dependent diabetes, you never want your insulin level to get too low. But you don't want to take too much insulin as this deprives the brain of energy, damaging the nerves. The better the metabolic control (correct levels of insulin and food), the longer the life expectancy for diabetics.

In Type II or non-insulin-dependent or adult-onset diabetes, the trouble is not too little insulin, but the failure of the cells to respond to insulin. Another name for this is insulin-resistant diabetes. This disease arises with the tendency of many people to put on weight as they age. It is a disease of inactivity and fat surplus. With enough fat stored away, the fat cells essentially get full. Once you are an adolescent, the number of fat cells you have is fixed; so if you put on weight the fat cells are bloated. Yet another heavy meal, a burst of insulin trying to promote more fat storage by the fat cells, and the fat cells refuse—'tough luck, I don't care if you are insulin; I am completely full'. The fat cells become less responsive to insulin. You may be confused at this time—if insulin regulates glucose uptake, why does it influence the amount of fat being stored in fat cells? For immensely complex and dense reasons (wet-towel-around-the head explanations), the storage of free fatty acids and glycerol as triglycerides requires glucose uptake. This decreased insulin sensitivity of the cells is mostly due to cells losing their specialized receptors for insulin, in response to the constant insulin signal.[1] This phenomenon is very much like that of teenage children who tune out the constant nagging from their parents!

Do the cells now starve? Of course not; the amount of fat stored in them was the source of the trouble in the first place. They get into trouble because of all that circulating glucose and fatty acids that are damaging the kidneys, blood vessels and the eyes.

How does stress affect this process? First, hormones of the stress response cause even more glucose and fatty acids to be mobilized in the bloodstream as we saw earlier.

Another subtler problem occurs with chronic stress. When something stressful happens, the brain directs the pancreas to stop producing insulin. It also seems that the brain does not quite trust the pancreas; so in a second step, the stress-response hormones act on fat cells to make them less sensitive to insulin. *Stress promotes insulin resistance.* When people

---

[1] As we saw in Section 3.2, this process is known as 'receptor down regulation'.

get into this state because they are taking large amounts of synthetic steroids, they have succumbed to 'steroid diabetes'.

Suppose you are in your mid-forties, overweight and just on the edge of insulin resistance. Along comes a period of chronic stress with those hormones repeatedly telling the cells that it is a great idea to be insulin resistant. Enough of this and you get diabetes!

For convenience, physicians usually use an absolute cut-off to decide when someone has insulin-resistant diabetes. Once you demonstrate a certain level of glucose during a glucose tolerance test, you get labelled as a diabetic. In reality, diabetes represents a continuum—there is no hard and fast point of insulin resistance at which the body suddenly gets into trouble. Instead, for every bit of insulin resistance there is a bit more of the risk of the type of damage discussed. People who are genetically susceptible have some sort of metabolic vulnerability, such that stress disrupts their metabolism to an atypical extent long before they become diabetic.

Diabetes more than doubles mortality and nearly triples the rate of heart diseases in men. It is one of the leading causes of blindness and in the top 10 causes of death. Unfortunately, the prevalence of Type II diabetes is increasing[2] and awareness of the causes and remedies is very poor in the general population.

---

[2] At the time of printing (year 2004) there are over 350 million diabetics in India and in the next 10 to 15 years, this number is expected to triple or quadruple.

| Chapter 5 | Heart Attacks | |

We saw in chapter 3 , that an important aspect of our body's stress response is the increase in cardiovascular output. The reason for this is not far to see. From the point of view of evolution, in the face of a physical stressor, oxygen and energy need to be diverted to muscles for flight or fight. The heart is the transport system pump; the delivery routes are the blood vessels. Using blood as the transporting medium, the heart propels oxygen, nutrients, wastes, and other substances to and past the body cells. Naturally, this (cardiovascular) output needs to be increased when faced with a stressor.

In simple terms, the heart works like an ordinary water pump—well, actually two pumps laid out side by side. The blood vessels are the 'pipes' that carry blood throughout the body. To give a very brief description, the right side of the heart works to pump impure blood to the lungs where it is purified and returned back to the left side of the heart. From there, it is pumped to the rest of the body through the arteries. When the body has depleted the oxygen in the blood, it is returned to the heart via the veins. For a more detailed description of the action of the heart, please refer to Appendix 3.

The question that comes to mind is how does the heart go about automatically pumping blood hour after hour, day after day? The answer lies in a special group of cells that have the ability to generate electrical activity on their own. These cells separate charged particles. Then they spontaneously leak certain charged particles into the cells. This produces electrical impulses in the pacemaker cells, which are spread over the heart, causing it to contract. These cells do this more than once per second to produce a normal rate of 72 beats per minute.

Who sets the rate at which the heart beats? The natural pacemaker of the heart is called the sinoatrial node (SA node). The heart also contains specialized fibres that conduct the electrical impulse from the pacemaker (SA node) to the rest of the heart.

Here is an interesting aside—the heart weighs only around 300 gm. An average heart pumps 70 ml per heartbeat. Assuming average heartbeats, the heart pumps 5 l per minute. Keeping the calculations going, it pumps 7,200 l per day or 18 million l by the time someone is 70 years old. That's not bad for a 300 gm pump!

To get additional output from a pump, you need to speed it up. In the case of the heart, it needs to beat faster and harder. In response to stress, the brain turns down the parasympathetic nervous system and turns up the sympathetic nervous system. The sympathetic nervous system triggers the heart's pacemaker to speed up resulting in faster heartbeats. The net result is an increase in the blood flow (both faster and with more force) from the heart. As can be expected, this process is far more complex than what is described here but the details are beyond the scope of this book. Typically, when we experience maximum stress, the blood flow is five times that of the normal flow.

Our body has another trick to increase the force with which the blood flows. Imagine for a moment, that you have a pipe through which water is flowing. If you would like to increase the force of the water but cannot increase the supply, you partly cover the mouth of the pipe with your finger. The narrowing of the opening causes the water to come out with force. This is the same trick that the body employs. Tiny circular muscles surround all the major arteries of the body. The sympathetic nervous system triggers those muscles to tighten (causing the arteries to narrow) and the blood pressure goes up. As a result of the constriction of the major arteries, blood is now being delivered with greater speed to the exercising muscles. At the same time, there is a dramatic decrease in the blood supply to the non-essential parts of the body including the blood supplied to the stomach, kidneys and the skin. This can explain the blanching or paleness observed in people under intense stress.

In a typical physical stressor (the scenario of the wounded animal running for life) there is loss of fluid—blood from the wound and sweat. Naturally, there is not enough time to drink the fluids required. If the blood volume goes down the oxygen and energy cannot be delivered to the muscles howsoever fast the heart may be beating. The body's stress response has another trick up its proverbial sleeve. It directs the kidneys to stop urine formation and reabsorb some of the water into the circulatory system. The messenger in this case is the hormone vasopressin. Needless to add, there are a whole lot of other hormones involved in regulating the water balance in the blood.

5.1 Effects of Chronic Stress

Repeated stress will cause extra work for the heart, the blood vessels and the kidneys. In simple terms, this will cause wear and tear of the system. Thus, repeated activation would cause fatigue and damage the heart and other major systems. Logically, we should then experience heart problems after many years and very late in life. We are all familiar with anecdotes about the incidence of heart diseases in younger people. In India, the incidences of cardiovascular diseases have gone up dramatically during the last two decades and this rise has been blamed on the modern lifestyle and stress. Unfortunately, we see that the cardiovascular diseases are showing up in even young and middle-aged people. How does repeated stress actually cause heart disease even in young people? In this section, we will take a closer look at the system to understand the source of the problem.

In order to appreciate the way stress response causes cardiovascular problems, we need to understand a little more about the blood vessels and how they can be damaged. A general feature of our circulatory system is that larger branches bifurcate into smaller branches and so on till we reach the tiny capillaries. This bifurcation is an extremely efficient way to organize the circulatory system and the net result is that no cell in the body is more than five cells away from a blood vessel. If you think about the number of cells in the human body[1] (approximately 100 trillion) you will realize that this

---

[1] How many cells are there in an adult human? Lots. More than anyone could count, and the bigger you are the more cells there would be. Growth

is no small accomplishment. Now for the really amazing part—the circulatory system represents less than 3 per cent of the total body mass!

The efficient circulatory system, however, has one major drawback. The points of bifurcation suffer from high forces as blood slams into it. These branch points are thus particularly vulnerable to injury. As we can imagine, if we increase the blood pressure, there will be greater turbulence to the flow and the branch points will experience even higher forces and will wear and tear and cause scarring of the arteries.

Recall from chapter 4 on metabolism, what the body does in the face of a stressor. It takes out money from the bank to pay for the defenses of the body—it releases triglycerides and glucose in the bloodstream. Now these globs of fat and glucose will stick to scarred and worn artery joints. In response to stress, the sympathetic nervous system increases the viscosity of blood by causing the blood platelets to clump. These clumps also stick to the arteries and add to the problem. Exacerbating the problems, cells full of fatty nutrients called foam cells begin to form there too. The arteries then clog and blood flow through them decreases. In scientific jargon it causes atherosclerosis. An accurate description of this phenomenon is the accumulation of plaque made of fats, starches, foam cells and calcium underneath the inner lining

---

is a process of cellular reproduction, so as you grow bigger you are made up of more cells. Following a similar logic, a larger person is larger because they have more cells, not because their cells are larger. In fact, cell types have a fairly uniform size across the entire human species.

of the blood vessels. Figure 5.1 shows an artery with atherosclerotic plaque. It shows how the plaque has narrowed the artery, thereby reducing the area available for the flow of blood.

Figure 5.1: Cross Section of Artery with Atherosclerotic Plaque

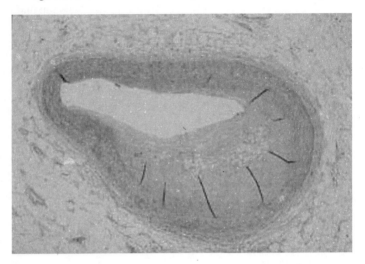

Now look at the ending of this drama—form enough plaque and restrict the blood flowing to the lower parts of the body. Your legs and chest will hurt like crazy whenever you walk due to lack of oxygen and glucose. You are a candidate for bypass surgery. If the same problem occurs for arteries going to the heart, you end up with coronary heart disease, and other horrible things. If you are really adventurous and have plaque in the arteries going to the brain you get a stroke—a brain thrombosis.

Now, for some more bad news. We have seen earlier how chronic stress messes your arteries and can lead to major problems in a short time. In times of stress, we have seen that the sympathetic nervous system increases the heart rate. The heart muscles require additional energy for performing this extra work and the body conveniently dilates the arteries supplying the heart muscles to divert more oxygen and glucose. The bad news is that in people with damaged arteries (specifically, plaque in the arteries going to the heart), the arteries instead of dilating now constrict! This is very different from the vasoconstriction described earlier in the chapter where some of the major arteries are constricted to increase blood pressure. Here we are talking of the small arteries that supply essentials to the heart that constrict instead of dilating. As a result, the heart is deprived of energy and oxygen just when it needs them the most (the scientific term for muscles being deprived of oxygen and nutrients is called ischemia). Your chest hurts like hell—scientific name for this condition is angina pectoris. Depressingly, it turns out that it takes only small periods of high blood pressure to cause the problem of contracting arteries.

The advent of modern imaging devices has allowed physicians to observe the working of the circulatory system at subtle levels. The surprising finding was that there were a number of episodes of heart artery contraction occurring all the time. Most of these episodes are painless (called silent episodes as they do not give out a warning signal of pain). Earlier, cardiologists warned you to be careful while undertaking physical activity if you had atherosclerosis. It appears that for such people trouble occurs all the time under normal psychological stress. It seems that the damaged system becomes very sensitive to stress whether physical or psychological. Each succeeding stressor makes the system more vulnerable till it all comes to a head with some cardiac catastrophe—the story of the person sitting or sleeping and being struck down by a sudden heart attack. It is incorrect to call it a 'sudden heart attack'. The drama has been playing out for a long time in the body as we have seen earlier. One of the most striking though unsurprising features of heart disease is that many times the catastrophe strikes during periods of extreme stress. Typical scenarios involve death of someone close, in the face of close personal danger, threat of a serious injury, and loss of status or self-esteem. The general consensus among cardiologists is that a sudden cardiac episode is an extreme version of acute stress causing heart ischemia coupled with ventricular fibrillation[2] or arrhythmia.[3]

Another story we have all heard is of people getting a heart attack after hearing of some major triumph or very happy news (winning an election, winning the lottery). This seems crazy. All the preceding discussion featured stress as the culprit and happiness does not fit into this category. If you pause to think for a moment, the idea does not seem far-fetched at all. Extreme joy and extreme fear obviously have different effects on the various parts of the body but for the

---

[2] In ventricular fibrillation, the ventricles of the heart begin to pump in a disorganized way so that they do not pump any blood.

[3] In ventricular arrhythmia the overall heartbeat becomes very irregular.

cardiovascular system the effects are roughly the same. Pounding your chest and wailing loudly or jumping up and down with joy place similar demands on the heart and can cause problems for the diseased heart. Think back to the definition of stress as any event that causes the body to be thrown out of allostatic balance. It does not matter in which direction the disruption takes place; it is the quantum of disruption that matters. Clearly, extreme joy causes the disruption to the allostatic equilibrium for the cardiovascular system just as extreme stress does.

Chapter 6	Does Stress Cause Ulcers?

While laying down the definition of stress in chapter 2, we looked at the experiments conducted by Selye who discovered the diseases of stress response when he found his laboratory rats developing ulcers. In common parlance, we use the term 'to get ulcers' as a way to indicate a stressful situation. In this chapter, we will take a closer look at the link between chronic stress, ulcers and some other diseases of the digestive system.

6.1 The Digestive System

Before we discuss the effects of stress on the formation of ulcers, we will take a brief look at the mechanical processes involved in digestion. Recall from our discussion on the digestive system from chapter 4, that it takes a huge amount of energy in terms of muscular movement to digest a stomach full of lunch. The food in the stomach is broken down mechanically and chemically. The stomach muscles contract violently on one side and the food is flung against the far sidewall of the stomach. This movement is called peristalsis. The small intestine is next in line and it goes through a series of directional contractions to push the food from one end to the other. After that the bowels do the same and the remainder is excreted. Circular muscles called sphincters are located at the end of the organs to make sure that things don't move to the next stage till the first stage is completed. The whole process relies on the ready availability of water to keep everything in solution. At the end of the cycle, in the large intestine, the water has to be absorbed again so that we are not dehydrated due to inadvertent excretion of the fluids. As you can imagine this entire process requires tremendous amount of energy. To put some numbers on it, *adults expend about 20 per cent of their daily energy on digestion!*

6.2 Stress Response

We will now take a look at the digestive system's response to stress. In the face of an acute physical stressor, it makes sense for the body to turn off all activities that consume a lot of energy and do not provide any immediate benefits. Digestion may be good in the long term by providing essential nutrients but it is useless in dealing with the immediate emergencies. The first step in the process is to stop the production of saliva as a result of which the mouth becomes dry. The stomach grinds to a halt; enzyme and acid secretion and contractions are stopped. The small intestine stops its movement and absorption does not take place. The blood flow to the digestive system is reduced and the blood delivers the oxygen and glucose to the exercising muscles where it is required. It all shows a superbly adapted system responding as expected to a stressor. So where is the problem?

Before we look at how repeated stressors can cause problems in the digestive system, it will help to know about one more process involved in digestion. Earlier, we saw how the muscular movement broke down food mechanically. The body uses another trick to break down food—the use of hydrochloric acid. This is a powerful acid and it breaks down virtually anything we eat—meats, vegetables, fats, refined foods, etc. The contractions help but the main weapon in the degradation is the hydrochloric acid. Even before this explanation is over, the alert reader would have noted something amiss. How come the acid does not degrade our own stomach? The answer is that the stomach has built layers and layers of protective mucous. The stomach has to expend a huge amount of effort to make sure that the acid does not affect its walls. This seems like a wonderful solution and digestion can proceed. Just to give an idea of the high level of protection, we see that there are at least six layers that protect the stomach from the acid.

Back to our original point on how stress causes problems with the digestive system. During a prolonged period of stress, digestion is frequently inhibited. To conserve energy, the stomach starts to economize and slows down the process of building the mucous walls. At the end of the stressor, when digestion resumes, the acid attacks the stomach walls—ulcer![1] An interesting point to note here is that the

---

[1] Ulcer is a common term in medicine that refers to a local defect or excavation of a surface of any organ or tissue that is produced by a sloughing of the inflammatory tissue. In this case we are talking about ulcers in the stomach and the correct term is *gastric ulcers*.

actual damage does not occur during the stressor but in the phase of recovering from the stressor. The obvious non-workable solution to avoid ulcers is to continue in the stressed condition! A more practical conclusion is that several periods of transient stress are worse than one prolonged period of stress from the point of view of ulcer formation.

Most experts agree that massive stressors like trauma, infections, accidents or burns can lead to the formation of stress ulcers just as described above. The difficulty is in explaining the ulcers that form over a period of time (emerging ulcers). There is an interesting story behind the discovery of the causes of emerging ulcers.

6.3 Do Bacteria Cause Ulcers?

In 1983, an Australian pathologist named Robert Warren discovered a bacterium called *helicobacter pylori*. He enlisted the help of his colleague Barry Marshall, who stated that this bacterium turned up consistently in the stomachs of people suffering from duodenal ulcers and stomach inflammation. He took a daring step and theorized that the bacterium actually caused the inflammation and the ulcer. He announced his findings at an international conference on gastroenterology and was promptly laughed out of the hall. Everyone knew that diet, stress, and genetic predisposition caused ulcers not some unknown bacterium. To further discredit his theory critics pointed out that the stomach is so acidic that no bacterium can survive there. Marshall countered by proving that *helicobacter pylori* did cause ulcers in laboratory mice. His experiments were promptly dismissed as being inapplicable to human conditions! In a heroic gesture worthy of any second rung Hindi movie, the mad scientist swallowed some bacteria and developed gastritis. Other researchers decided to conduct additional studies and they found that he was absolutely right. It turns out that *helicobacter pylori* do live in the acidic stomach. It protects itself with a coating that is acid resistant and further wraps itself in a coat of bicarbonate. This bacterium probably explains over 80 per cent of the cases of ulcers in western populations.

In the developing world nearly 100 per cent of the people are infected by this bacterium but not all suffer from ulcers. It is probably the most chronic bacterial infection in humans. The bacterium infects cells lining the stomach wall and cause gastritis. This compromises the ability of the cells to defend against the stomach acid—and you end up with an ulcer in the duodenal wall. Many details are being sorted out but the greatest triumph for the two Australians has been the near universal adoption of their theory. It has now become common to treat ulcers with antibiotics like amoxycillin. Best of all, various studies have shown that ulcers can be cured and the infection does not recur.

Now for the interesting postscript. Only 10 per cent of the people infected with the bacteria get an ulcer. It means that there is some other agent in addition to the bacterium that causes ulcers. The consensus seems to be that stress by itself does not cause ulcers. Rather, stress worsens the impact of *helicobacter pylori* infection and that leads to ulcers. Repeated studies have shown that in humans, ulceration is likely to occur in people who are anxious, depressed, or undergoing severe life stressors. Some very sophisticated studies coupled with equally complicated statistical analysis have shown that in the case of massive infections with *helicobacter pylori*, even moderate stressors can cause ulcers. In the case of massive stressors, even a minor infection is enough to cause ulcers.

Chapter 7	Personality Type and Temperament

We have noted that stress response can be modulated by various psychological factors. Many scientific studies have demonstrated that an individual faced with a psychological stressor will exhibit less of a stress response when given an outlet for frustration, a sense of control over events and predictive information. This topic will be covered in detail in chapter 14.

This finding is fine for laboratory settings where such experiments are conducted. In real life, we all differ in the way we react to different events and use various psychological factors to modulate stress response. Our use of various psychological factors to respond to different stressors can be defined as our personality. Coupled with our personality is our temperament. How do we view the world? Is every interaction with other people a hostile one? In ambiguous circumstances, do we always find the worst news? How good are we at building long-term relationships and friendships? Can we rely on our social network in times of crisis? Some people are very good at using various psychological variables to modulate their stress response and consequently they are less prone to stress-related disease.

7.1 Personality Type of Managers?

In this chapter we will look at one particular personality type and see what the consequences are in terms of vulnerability to stress-related diseases. Though the picture is grim for such people, there is definite good news—the proverbial silver lining to the dark cloud. Such personality traits are not permanent and you can make an active effort to change, which reduces your vulnerability.

It is not usually difficult to spot people with this particular personality type. It is even easier to meet them in the higher rungs of the competitive corporate world. They are immensely competitive, aggressive, under time pressure, impatient and hostile. These are the traits that have been rewarded in the corporate world and they have reached high positions. I was reminded of this when standing in line at a bank ATM. There was a very small queue of three people and the well-dressed executive in front of me was getting upset. In the few minutes that it took for his turn to come, he was tapping his foot, muttering under his breath about slow people who should not use ATMs and must have looked at his watch at least 10 times. No, he was not impatient because he had to rush to a hospital to save a life! For such people it does not matter how important or trivial their work is. They are concerned about doing things on time and with the greatest possible speed.

The fascinating story of how this personality type came to be identified as the one that ran the greatest risk of contracting diseases, begins in the 1950s. Two successful cardiologists Friedman and Rosenman were facing an unexpected problem in their office. The chairs in their waiting room were being worn out quickly and had to be reupholstered every few months. Being busy cardiologists, they could not be bothered by such a small problem but the chairs continued to show immense wear and tear. No doubt there were frequent clashes between their office manager and the upholsterer about the quality of work. One day, a new upholsterer took a look at the chairs and made a simple observation—what is wrong with your patients? People don't wear out chairs in this way. It was not difficult to see what he meant. Only the front section and the arms of the chairs were worn out. It was as if all the patients were sitting on the edge of their chair and plucking at the arms of the chair. Of course, nobody paid the slightest attention to what the upholsterer was saying. If Dr Friedman and Rosenman listened to him it made no impact on them. It was four or five years later and the formal research conducted by Dr Friedman and Dr Rosenman began to show the role of personality in cardiovascular disease that everyone was suddenly reminded about the upholsterer and his observation about the wear pattern. Interesting postscript—to this day, no one seems to remember the name of the upholsterer!

So, what was this fascinating study conducted by Friedman and Rosenman? They observed that many of their coronary patients exhibited some common personality traits—immensely competitive, over-achieving, impatient, under time pressure and hostile. Later they named this personality as Type A. Their initial observation was met with a lot of scepticism but their next study was well accepted. In that prospective study they started out with healthy individuals and examined whether having a Type A personality increased the risk of coronary disease. Surprisingly, they discovered that Type A personality was a huge risk factor for coronary disease; the risk was almost equal to that presented by other factors like smoking or high cholesterol levels.

This was accepted by the medical community and was given a lot of publicity by the popular press at that time. Several carefully conducted studies after that failed to establish such a link! It seemed as if being Type A was not a risk factor after all. To make matters worse for Dr Friedman and Dr Rosenman, other studies showed that having Type A personality actually helped in recovering from coronary disease and indicated better chances of survival.

Recent analysis of the original data and other studies have identified the characteristic from Type A personality which is the main risk factor. It turns out to be hostility. The same results were found in a large prospective study of doctors conducted over a period of 25 years. It discovered that a high degree of hostility predicted a greater chance of coronary disease. Newer studies with a number of different groups of people, have confirmed the same basic finding—hostility predicts a high degree risk of coronary disease, atherosclerosis and higher risk of death from these diseases.

Some notable scientists disagree with this view, the chief among them being Dr Friedman. They argue that the core of hostility is a sense of being under time pressure and the basis for that is rampant insecurity. Their work suggests that a persistent sense of insecurity is, in fact, a better predictor of coronary disease.

Therefore, what is the latest research on this subject? A huge prospective study started in 1985 in the US tracked people for 15 years. The aim was to uncover the risk of cardiovascular diseases associated with these Type A traits viz.—time urgency, impatience, hostility and achievement striving competitiveness. The results published in 2003 confirm previous studies *that both hostility and time urgency are associated with higher risk of cardiovascular diseases within 15 years. These results are independent of age, sex, race, alcohol consumption, body weight and physical activity.* This is a remarkable finding and we need to focus on changing these two aspects in our personalities. Another thing to note from this study is that striving for achievement and competitiveness do not have any effect on the risk for heart diseases. So don't worry if you are highly competitive and are working hard to achieve your goals.

7.2 Hostility and Risk of Cardiovascular Disease

As far as hostility is concerned, it is not clear which type is bad. Is it the overt hostility (all lawyers watch out—you may be at higher risk of coronary disease!) or is it the repressive type (the tendency not to express your emotions when angry)? There are contradictory studies, which favour the different viewpoints. One fascinating study seems to give a better picture. In that study, healthy volunteers were shown a film clip that evokes some strong emotions (like a surgical procedure with blood and all the internals). The volunteers showed strong signs of sympathetic nervous system activation (stress response). Another set of volunteers was shown the same clip but they were instructed beforehand not to display their emotions. After the film, this group had a higher stress response than the group who were not prevented from expressing their emotions. Thus, repression tends to exaggerate the intensity of the stress response.

Irrespective of which type of hostility is more harmful, the interesting question is why should hostility cause a greater risk of coronary disease? Some interesting studies will help us find the answer. First, a group of hostile and non-hostile people was given some math problems to solve (non-social stressor). Nothing exciting and both groups had roughly the same stress response. Now, throw in some social provocation (like being repeatedly interrupted during the test, loud noises in the background) and every time, the hostile people had a high stress response. They were dumping the hormones epinephrine, norepinephrine in their bloodstream and showed elevated blood pressure.

A number of similar experiments have been conducted with different settings and different social stressors. They all point to the higher stress response in hostile people. Subjectively, we can say that hostile people get angry over incidents that most of us would ignore or find mildly provocative. For the hostile (anxious) people, life is full of menacing situations that demand constant vigilance and a particularly hostile response. They probably go through life viewing the world as full of provocations that everyone else does not find bothersome.

For all the reasons we discussed in chapter 5 on stress response and the cardiovascular system, these people will be ideal candidates for coronary disease.

At the beginning of the chapter, I pointed out an important caveat when talking about personality types—that *having a specific personality type increases your risk of coronary disease but that you can change your personality and reduce your risk.* If such people reduce their hostility through therapy or their own efforts, their risk of heart disease goes down. Put simply, the hostile people are not being nice to those around them. In non-scientific terms, they should strive to be nicer and bring a smile to the faces of those around them. It will have a positive impact on their own lives.

7.3 The Vulcans

In my errant youth, I was fascinated by a TV serial called 'Star Trek' and repeatedly watched the episodes of that show. For those uninitiated in the field of junk science fiction TV shows, the story line of Star Trek is roughly as follows—a group of intrepid space travellers use a space ship propelled by novel technology to explore the universe. The captain is a human and he has a diverse bunch of aliens acting as his crew. The first officer of the ship is a Vulcan—a human-like species. The Vulcans though human in appearance have complete control over their emotions. They operate solely on logic in all matters and are completely unruffled by emotional turmoil around them. It seems that in the distant past the Vulcans were a very emotional race and fought endless wars before they mastered the technique of controlling their emotions.

Well, the whole point of bringing Star Trek trivia in this book is that there are some people whom we meet everyday who have a good degree of control over their emotions. The correct scientific terminology for describing their personality is repressive. They appear calm in everything they do. They seem to have their life ordered and we sometime wish that we would have their nature. They don't appear to have many stressors; they describe themselves as successful and accomplished. Interestingly, it is not just their feelings but studies have shown such people to be successful and accomplished in their fields. So, what is the problem? It turns out that these people show an elevated stress response. They have glucocorticoids levels similar to those of anxious people and they show increased sympathetic activation. Interestingly, these people show no symptoms of being anxious. In fact, the opposite is true and they appear to lead a pretty disciplined life. So how do they do it? Research has revealed that such people have extra activity in an area of the brain that inhibits emotion—the frontal cortex. This is the area that inhibits impulsive behaviour and cognition. Modern imaging techniques have shown that repressive people have unusually high activity in the frontal area when stressed. It seems like their brain is working overtime to regain control and retain their balance. Ultimately these individuals pay the price for all their order and discipline. The extra stress-response hormones and activity of the sympathetic system result in lowered immunity and a greater risk of cardiovascular disease. I wonder if the same problems affect the Vulcans?

Chapter 8 | Stress and Reproduction

In this chapter, we will examine the role of the various stress-response hormones as they relate to reproduction. First, we will take a look at the male reproductive system. Your average male has a pretty run of the mill system as compared to the complexity of the female reproductive system.

As always, things start in the brain, which releases the hormone LHRH.[1] This stimulates the pituitary to release the two hormones leutenizing hormone (LH) and follicle stimulating hormone (FSH). LH stimulates the testes to release testosterone. Lacking eggs and follicles, in males the FSH stimulates sperm production. Stress disrupts this process at each stage. The first casualty is the LHRH. With the onset of stress, the endorphins and enkephalins act to block the release of LHRH from the brain. Another hormone released during stress reduces the sensitivity of the pituitary to LHRH. This is an attack on both flanks—less of LHRH production and lower sensitivity of the pituitary to LHRH. The LHRH concentrations decline which results in the decline in levels of LH and FSH. As a result, the testes stop functioning

---

[1] LHRH stands for leutenizing hormone releasing hormone.

and the level of testosterone declines. Further, glucocorticoids block the response of the testes to LH. The decline in the level of circulating hormone is only part of the problem. The actual problem is that stress causes difficulties in getting erections. Put simply, for the male to have an erection, it is necessary to have the parasympathetic system active. As we saw in chapter 3, stress causes the sympathetic system to be activated and the parasympathetic system to be blocked. This makes it difficult to get erections during periods of stress resulting in impotence. Even if the male can get an erection, it is difficult to sustain the erection during a stressor.

8.1 Female Reproductive System

The first step in the female reproductive system is the same as in the males. LHRH is released by the brain, which causes the pituitary to release LH and FSH. In the case of females, the FSH as the name implies, stimulates the follicles. In the first half of the menstrual cycle (to use the scientific jargon—the follicular stage), levels of LHRH, LH and FSH and estrogen build up leading to ovulation. This starts the second phase of the cycle (called the luteal phase). The dominant hormone in this phase is progesterone,[2] which is made in the ovary. It stimulates the uterine walls to mature, so that if an egg is fertilized, it can implant in the wall and develop into an embryo. Unlike the male reproductive system,

---

[2] The name of this hormone will ring a bell with some women who needed to take extremely painful progesterone injections during IVF or other assisted reproductive procedures.

the levels of the hormones vary with time and the process is a lot more complicated. Not surprisingly, the portion of the brain that controls the hormone release (hypothalamus) is structurally more complicated in women than men.

One of the interesting facets of reproduction is the eggs and their storage. It is incredible that the lifetime supply of eggs is formed even before birth![3] While the female foetus is developing, between months three and six the eggs are formed. It is only after she grows up and has hit puberty that these eggs are released. Evolution has worked a surprisingly smart way to store these eggs.

Many of the mechanisms that disrupt the male reproductive system, also affect the female system. Endorphins and enkephalins will inhibit LHRH release and the glucocorticoids will block pituitary sensitivity to LHRH. This will result in lowered LH, FSH and estrogen release thereby lengthening the follicular stage. This will extend the whole cycle and make it irregular. An extreme version of this is a condition termed anovulatory amenorrhea where the entire ovulatory system is shut down.

Another way in which stress affects the reproductive system is by suppressing progesterone, which disrupts the maturation of the uterine walls. Worse, prolactin, which is released during stress, interferes with the working of progesterone. This is a double whammy. First, the ovulatory hormones are affected, thereby reducing the chances of ovulation. If an egg

---

[3] A human female typically has about 400,000 follicles/potential eggs, all formed before birth. Only several hundred of these 'eggs' will actually ever be released during her reproductive years.

does ovulate and get fertilized there is very little chance of it to implant normally.

An interesting aside on the hormone prolactin. It is a very versatile hormone and besides stress it is released during breastfeeding and is an effective contraceptive. There is a reflex loop that goes from the nipples to the hypothalamus. If there is nipple stimulation for any reason, the hypothalamus signals the pituitary to secrete prolactin. Have sufficient prolactin over a long period of time in the blood and you have a very effective contraceptive. Hence, the conventional wisdom that breastfeeding your baby is a good contraceptive. Like all ideas floating around in the garb of 'conventional wisdom' it is partially true. In the remark on the contraceptive effects of prolactin, the key point to note is the phrase 'long period of time'. At the start of breastfeeding, prolactin is released but ceases with the end of feeding. As the average mother nurses her baby only for five or six times during a day, the sustained levels of prolactin are not maintained and the contraceptive effect is not seen at all times.

There is a surprising facet to the female reproductive system and the effect that stress has on it. Typically, there is a small amount of male sex[4] hormone in the bloodstream of women. This hormone does not come from the ovaries but from the adrenal glands (hence the not surprising name—adrenal androgens). The amount is a small fraction of that found in males and an enzyme in the fat cells of females

---

[4] It is incorrect to use terms like 'male sex hormone' as all hormones are present in males and females. It is only the quantity that differs between the sexes.

usually eliminates these androgens by converting them into estrogen. In the face of physical stressor when the body weight drops and fat stores are depleted, this conversion is affected and the level of androgens builds up. The androgens disrupt many steps in the female reproductive system. As would be obvious, this happens if you starve voluntarily—as in the case of young teenage girls chasing the impossible dream of being as pencil thin as supermodels. In such cases, the loss of fat cells leading to androgen buildup results in impaired reproduction mechanisms. In young girls puberty can be delayed for years and in older women cycles can become irregular or cease altogether.

Harking back to one of the main themes of this book, the stress response that disrupts the female reproductive system and prevents pregnancies is very logical from the evolutionary point. An average pregnancy costs over 50,000 calories and such an undertaking should not be undertaken during periods of stress or when reserves of energy are not available in the fat cells.

8.2 High-tech Pregnancy and High Failure Rates

Infertility! The dreaded malady has almost no match in terms of its ability to cause stress, disrupt relationship between husband and wife, high rates of depression, inability to concentrate at work and estrangement from family and friends. For those unfortunate enough to have to face this condition, it seems to be the worst thing that can happen! Typically, the most common problems faced are the damage to the relationships with friends and relatives who have children. As people in similar age groups move on and have families, the infertile couple finds life getting harder with every baby shower, birthday party or those occasions where families get together. In many areas of the country, it is common practice to exclude childless women from religious functions involving babies. The second problem is more intimate and concerns the relationship between the wife and husband when lovemaking gets turned into a medical procedure and that too an unsuccessful one!

In this scenario of doom and gloom there is a ray of sunshine in terms of the medical advances in the field of assisted reproductive techniques (commonly abbreviated as ARTs). Terms such as artificial insemination, donor eggs, sperm donor and *in-vitro* fertilization are even beginning to show up in the popular press. These techniques represent a tremendous advance and can help a number of couples facing infertility. The field has advanced to such an extent and the techniques are used so commonly that many governments are faced with the task of updating the laws and regulations on such basic issues as definitions of parents! A recent case in the UK highlights this problem. It concerned a couple that had their fertilized embryos frozen and stored. Unfortunately, the couple separated and a few years later the woman wanted to use those embryos to have a baby. The husband objected and claimed that he had as much right over the use of the embryos as his ex-wife. When last heard, the courts had ruled in favour of the husband though the case is likely to go all the way to the European courts and many other cases are likely to come up.

Going back to the start of this section where we mentioned the stressfulness of infertility. For those undergoing the high-tech reproductive procedures, the problem gets worse. These procedures themselves are very stressful. Numerous tests, weeks of painful hormone injections and hormone suppressors, daily sonograms, constant worry over details like number of follicles, their size and location and the emotional roller coaster of whether the day's news is good or bad. The dramatic changes in hormone levels caused by the injections also affect the mood and mental state. At the end of all this, the actual procedure and then the wait to find out if things have worked out. Unfortunately, the success rates are very low and many times the whole cycle has to start all over again. The maximum success rate for such an IVF cycle is something like 10 per cent to 15 per cent. It is interesting to note that we do not know the success rate for natural pregnancy. The body may have a number of natural attempts that fail but they are not measured. An intrusive, time-consuming and painful procedure like IVF, however, does not have high success rates. Patients go through it, as they do not have any other options. Another fact to note is that such procedures and the associated medications are horrendously expensive. A typical IVF cycle costs approximately Rs 80,000[5] and it is not uncommon to have five or six attempts.

---

[5] These figures should be taken as indicative rather than definitive. The costs will vary dramatically and change every year. No doubt in a few years, after publication, this number would be useless. Nevertheless, I give that figure to emphasize the fact that the toll of these procedures is both emotional and financial. A young couple shortly after marriage is not going to find such expenses easy to manage with their own resources.

The previous discussions should be enough to convince anyone that the assisted reproductive techniques are stressful and they may contribute to the problem of infertility. A number of researchers have examined this problem to determine if the stress from the procedure causes low success rates. There are some indications that increased stress during the procedure leads to lower success rates. A caveat is in order here. These studies are not very rigorous and the answers should not be taken as definitive till more rigorous and comprehensive studies are done. The chief problem is that these studies were carried out in women undergoing some assisted reproductive procedure. Their infertility ensures that they are stressed (whether the stress is exacerbated by the procedure or not) and they are likely to have low success rates. Having said that it is still important to note that stress does disrupt the reproductive system and can reduce the chance for pregnancy. It may be obvious, but some of the stress management techniques discussed in later chapters should be employed by such couples to improve their chances of success. Just my two bits worth, it would be a nice advance in medical science, if the techniques improved to such an extent that they eliminated the stress and dramatically improved the rate of success.

8.3 A Nuanced View

The preceding sections would convince any reader that the female reproductive system is quite complex and susceptible to disruption at many stages. Some of the villains include depletion of fat cells, secretions of endorphins, prolactin, glucocorticoids, lack of progesterone and excessive prolactin interfering with the progesterone. It seems likely that even mild stressors should disrupt the system. Now take a look around you—grinding poverty, families with nursing mothers living below flyovers and bridges. Horrible (some would even call them inhuman) living conditions, diseases too numerous to enumerate, no place to live, no jobs, no food—you name it and that stressor exists. Yet, you see that children are being born and raised. No doubt there is high infant mortality but the key point is that the reproductive system is still working. A set of horrendous studies conducted by Nazi doctors on women in concentration camps showed that almost half of them stopped ovulating within a month of their being imprisoned in the concentration camps. That finding should come as no surprise—mental and physical torture, extreme deprivation and inhuman living conditions will surely take a toll. The more interesting fact to note is that the other half continued to ovulate!

It seems that the reproductive system is truly robust and can withstand a lot of stress. My personal belief is that it comes from the fact that reproduction is one of the basic instincts and evolution has favoured a system that can continue to work in the face of a number of odds. The survival instinct triumphs in the end! I hope that this will give a small ray of hope to the infertile couples and they are able to focus on the resilience of the reproductive systems.

Chapter 9	The Immune System	

Inside our body there is an amazing protection mechanism called the immune system. It is designed to defend us against the millions of bacteria, microbes, viruses, toxins and parasites that would love to invade our body. To understand the power of the immune system, all that we have to do is look at what happens to anything once it dies. That sounds vulgar, but it does show you something very important about the immune system. When something dies its immune system (along with everything else) shuts down. Within hours, all sorts of bacteria, microbes, and parasites invade the body. None of these things are able to get in when our immune system is working, but the moment the system collapses the invasion begins. It takes these organisms only a few weeks to completely dismantle a dead body and carry it away, until all that's left is a skeleton. Obviously our immune system is doing something amazing to keep all of that dismantling from happening when we are alive!

More than a 100 years ago, scientists did a simple experiment. They used a group of volunteers who were allergic to a flower. During a series of tests, it was demonstrated that an artificial flower triggered the allergic reaction just like the real one did. It seemed that the brain could influence the working of the immune system. In a more recent study conducted on professional actors[1] they were required to do either a tragic scene or a happy one. The ones doing the tragic scene showed a stress response with decreased immune function. In contrast, the actors who were doing an euphoric scene showed an improvement in their immune response. It seems clear that the brain can poke its proverbial nose into the affairs of the immune system. How does the brain go about meddling in the immune system? The autonomic nervous system sends nerves into the tissues that form or store the cells of the immune system that end up in the blood circulation. Further, the tissues of the immune system are sensitive to all the hormones released by the pituitary.[2] Studies such as these clearly show the strong link between the nervous system and the immune system. The obvious conclusion is that stress can alter the immune functions. To appreciate the role of stressors in disrupting the immune system, we need to take a look (as is the case in this book, it will be a brief look) at the functioning of the immune system and then analyse the functioning during stress.

---

[1] As you would have guessed, this study was done at the Mecca of the film industry, Hollywood (actually, it was done at The University of California at Los Angeles).

[2] The pituitary in only a lackey of the brain and is under the direct control of the brain.

9.1 Functioning of the Immune System

The main function of the immune system is to fight infectious agents such as viruses, bacteria, parasites and fungi. To get an idea of the enormous complexity of this task, first think about what the immune system should not do—attack the body's own self. Somehow, the system should be able to distinguish between 'self' and 'non-self'. Every time it sees a non-self cell, the immune system has to attack it. Obviously, it needs to remember such foreigners and how they look to be ready to face the next attack from the same organism. The best way to think of the immune system is to view it as an army defending the nation. The problems of the real army like logistics, transportation, supplies, etc., are all present in the immune army too.

The foot soldiers in the immune army are the white blood cells. There are two types of white blood cells—lymphocytes and monocytes. Lymphocytes are further classified as T cells and B cells which are formed in the bone marrow. The T cells mature in the thymus and the B cells mature in the bone marrow; hence, the unsurprising choice of the prefix 'T' or 'B'. There are several types of T cells that perform different functions and have different designations like T helper, T suppressor, etc.

The job of the lookout in the immune army goes to the monocytes. When an infectious agent invades the body, it is a macrophage[3] (a type of monocyte) that recognizes the foreign particle. The macrophage presents the evidence to the T-helper

---

[3] Macrophage literally means big eater.

cell. The macrophage also releases a substance called interleukin-1 that stimulates the activity of the T-helper cell. The T-helper cells now sound the metaphorical alarm by releasing interleukin-2. In response to the alarm the T cells begin to proliferate. The result of all this activity is that another type of white blood cells called cytotoxic-killer cells begin to proliferate and attack and destroy the infectious agent.[4] In scientific jargon, the T cells cause cell-mediated immunity.

The B cells fight the infection in a different manner from that described earlier. A simplified model of how the immune system fights off a virus using the B cells is given below. Any infectious agent that enters the body will eventually be taken up in the lymph system.

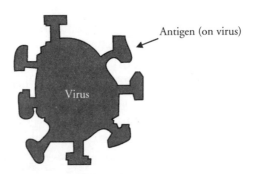

Antigen (on virus)

Virus

This may happen soon after infection, or it may not happen until the invader has found a niche and begun to replicate. In one of your lymph nodes, the infectious agent will meet a macrophage. The macrophage will ingest the invader.

---

[4] It is the T-cell component of the immune system that is disabled by the AIDS virus.

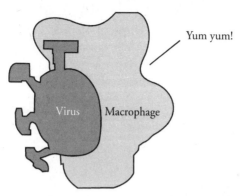

Yum yum!

Virus   Macrophage

Then the macrophage takes the invader apart, and displays the viral antigens on its surface for other immune cells to read.

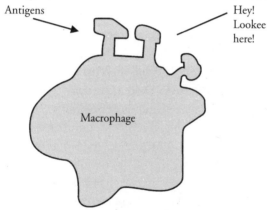

Antigens

Hey!
Lookee
here!

Macrophage

Antigens are proteins specific to each particular micro-organism. The antigens act as an identity card that allows our immune system to recognize invader organisms that need to be eliminated. After displaying the agent's antigens, the macrophage will send out a message to a T-helper cell to read and recognize the antigens.

Once the T cell has read the antigens, it will send out messages to activate the B cells, which will in turn come and read the antigens from the macrophage's surface.

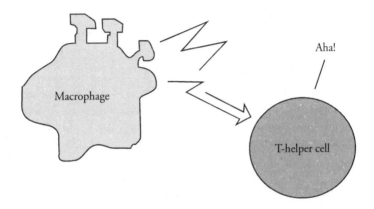

The activated B cell will then produce millions of antibodies. The antibody is a protein that will bind with an antigen. Each antibody is unique and specific; for example, a polio antibody will only bind with a polio virus. We produce antibodies because, given the high concentration of infectious agent that is needed to cause a disease, our macrophages could not go after the invaders alone. However, antibodies will outnumber the invaders and will effectively help us get rid of them.

How do the antibodies bind with the infectious agent? The antibody resembles the mirror image of the antigen (like a key and a lock), usually providing such a close fit that, if they bump into each other, the antibody will grab the antigen without letting it go. Once an antibody has locked with

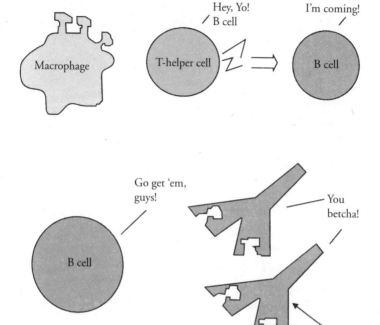

an invader, it will broadcast a signal that says, 'eat me and whatever I have captured'. A macrophage will in turn get the message and will devour the antibody-antigen complex and rid the body of the infectious agent.

To hark back to our original description of a nation's army, the communication and logistics is a very critical component of success and the case of the immune system is no different. The system is distributed throughout the circulatory system and needs reliable mechanisms for communication. The immune system uses chemical messengers that are

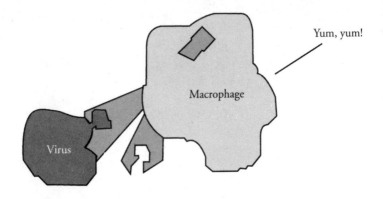

Yum, yum!

Macrophage

Virus

transported by the blood. We briefly mentioned some of them—interleukin-1 and -2 and the B-cell growth factor. As you can expect, the system is far more complex than outlined in this brief overview. For example, there are at least six other interleukins with specialized functions. There are other classes of messengers like the interferons that activate the lymphocytes (an area we have not discussed).

I can picture to myself the macrophages going about their daily duty. As they are patrolling the body, they see the boring liver cells. Ignore and move on. Ha! suspicious activity near the stomach. No, false alarm, it is only the boring stomach cells. A little further out there—found an invader! Attack, send out the alarm.... What happens when something goes wrong with this process? Either the macrophages do not identify the invaders or worse yet, attack the body cells. The latter results in horrible autoimmune diseases—rheumatoid arthritis (joints are attacked), juvenile diabetes (pancreatic cells are attacked), multiple sclerosis (nerve cells are attacked).

9.2 Effects of Stress on the Immune System

Recall the story of Selye and his ulcerated rats. There was brief mention of shrunken thymus gland. It turns out that the best documented way in which immune suppression occurs is via the glucocorticoids. These stress-response hormones have a pretty wide area of influence in the immune system. They cause the shrinkage of the thymus, inhibit the release of the messengers interleukin and interferons and they make circulating lymphocytes less sensitive to infectious alarms. The glucocorticoids cause the lymphocytes to be pulled out of circulation and even worse can actually kill them. Some other stress-response hormones also suppress immunity (like beta-endorphins) though their role is far from clear and the effect is far less than that of glucocorticoids.

The alert reader at this point may ask why the immune system is suppressed during stress? All along, we have been emphasizing that the body's stress response has evolved superbly to fight physical stressors. So, why has evolution favoured a system that seems to knock out the immune system when faced with a stressor? Logically, it does not make sense to lower your guard when faced with a stressor. In fact, it seems the opposite should be true. One of the things we noted was that during a stressor, long-term tasks that involve expenditure of energy are shut off (digestion, ovulation and so on). In that light, consider what the body does to the immune system—it expends energy to actively dismantle the immune system when it ought to be spending energy to shore up the defences.

The story of the immune system and stress is actually pretty complicated. Newer techniques, particularly in developing extremely sensitive tests to determine levels of hormones have led to a nuanced picture of what happens to the immune system in response to stress. First, as expected, the immune system is enhanced at the onset of stress (see Figure 9.1). For the first 30 minutes or so of a stressor, the immune system is enhanced. After about 60 minutes, with sustained release of glucocorticoids and the workings of the sympathetic system, the immune system starts to be suppressed. If the stressor is of moderate duration, the net effect is that the immune system is brought back to the pre-stress level. No harm done. It is only in the face of chronic stress that the suppression of the immune system is such that it goes below the pre-stress level. Again, it reinforces the major theme of this book. It is the chronic stress and the body's response to it that causes the problems. Alert readers will ask as to why the immune system should be brought down from the high level it had reached during stress? Is it not good for the body to have the immune system working in top gear? The first obvious answer is that it would be too costly—the effort required to keep the immune system at an enhanced level will require a considerable expenditure of energy.[5] The second explanation is that a chronically activated immune system becomes even more active, spiraling out of control and leading to autoimmune diseases.

_____

[5] Not very different from the face-off in 2002 between India and Pakistan when both armies were put in combat-ready state along their borders for almost nine months taking a huge toll in human and monetary terms.

Figure 9.1: Immune Response Under Stress

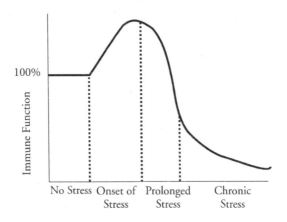

To summarize—

- During stress, the stress-response hormones cause a transient activation of the immune system.
- Stress response enhances the immune defences and helps in redistributing them to the site of the infection.
- To avoid the danger of overshooting into autoimmunity, exposure to glucocorticoids brings the immune system back to the pre-stress level.

In the case of chronic stress and prolonged glucocorticoids release, the immune system is suppressed below normal levels. These findings help to explain some facets of the autoimmune disease and increased vulnerability to infections as will be discussed in subsequent sections.

9.3 Heavy Exercise and Infections

A quick recap, at the onset of stress, there is a transient activation of the immune system. So, for those who exercise regularly (stressing the body mildly) there is a beneficial effect in terms of improved immune functioning. Just because a little of something is good, it does not mean that a lot of it will be better. This point is brought home in a study that examined the excessive rates of throat infections seen in athletes involved in heavy training. The graph in Figure 9.2 shows the effects of training on the risk of throat infections. As you

Figure 9.2: Training Load and Risk of Throat Infection

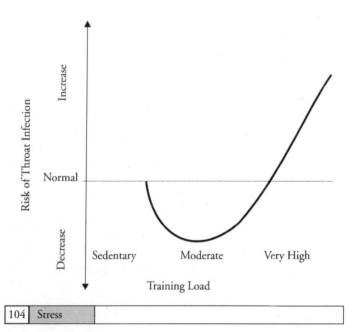

can see heavy training (chronic stress) causes a rise in the risk of infection (due to suppression of the immune system). Note the beneficial effect of moderate exercise—the risk of infection is the lowest (enhanced immune system).

9.4 Treatment of Autoimmune Diseases with Steroids

Autoimmune diseases are caused by an overactive immune system attacking the body; it is logical that suppressing the immune system will reduce the disease. That is precisely what happens when such patients are given massive amounts of glucocorticoids. The net result is less damage from the autoimmune disease but at the cost of a suppressed immune system. Such patients are obviously more at risk from other diseases and have to be vigilant.

Paradoxically, many patients report that their autoimmune diseases deteriorate in times of stress. It is easy to dismiss this effect as psychosomatic as it is clear that the glucocorticoids will suppress the immune system and hence the autoimmune disease should get better, not worse. For a number of years, this was the prevalent attitude among physicians. A number of studies have demonstrated the link between stress and worsening of the symptoms autoimmune disease. As we saw in Figure 9.1, the answer is obvious. The onset of stress enhances the immune systems functioning making the autoimmune disease worse. Repeated moderate daily stressors will cause a worsening of the condition. Also, chronic stress with the long-term release of glucocorticoids will suppress the immune system. For obvious reasons, getting stressed cannot be a treatment option for people suffering from autoimmune diseases!

The entire field of immune functioning and stress is relatively new and there are a lot of tentative findings. We can outline the basic facts as—

- We are subjected to different stressors both in terms of frequency and duration. The stress pattern will determine the level of our stress response.
- The magnitude and duration of the stress response will determine the level at which the immune system functions.
- The level of functioning of our immune system determines what diseases we get and how we fight off infections.

There are many subtleties involved in the simple steps outlined above. We will look at some specific cases where there is a link between stress and diseases associated with immune system dysfunction. To understand this linkage, we will only look at those instances where these linkages have been conclusively established in proper scientific studies.

9.5 Social Isolation

This is one of the extreme forms of stress that a human being can be subjected to. Evolution has favoured us with a large number of tools like language, emotions, and a hugely developed brain; that makes social cohesion possible and even necessary. It is obvious that depriving a person of this basic human requirement is a cruel punishment. No wonder, even the most hardened criminals dread the prospect of 'solitary confinement'. Social interactions can have a positive effect and would be one of the strategies employed for stress reduction. We explore this idea further in chapter 14 on stress management techniques. It should come as no surprise that other primates exhibit the same need for social interaction.

A large number of studies have demonstrated that social isolation for long periods leads to immune suppression and diseases associated with such suppression. Many of those studies were prospective—that is they were tracking people before the social isolation and then studied the results afterwards. These studies are extremely time consuming and costly. The short cut is to find people suffering from the disease and then ask them about the stressful things in their lives (retrospective studies). The obvious drawback is that human memory is very unreliable when it comes to suffering. When sick, we tend to exaggerate the conditions that we think may have caused the disease. So it helps to have prospective studies where such bias of human memory has been removed. Such studies have confirmed a strong link between stress and immune suppression.

The fewer social relationships a person has, the shorter the life expectancy and higher the impact of various infectious diseases. In medical terms, a relationship can take any form—marriage, friendship, religious affiliation and belonging to organized groups. In particular, separation from a spouse or facing severe marital difficulties is associated with worse immune functioning. Other studies have found that people who are very lonely (measured in scientific terms on a loneliness scale) have been found to have relatively higher depressed immune systems and higher risk of death.

Therefore, we find a lot of scientific literature on the subject that affirms the idea that social isolation leads to higher immune suppression. The obvious question to ask is how big is this impact on the chances of getting disease? The answer is that it is a very big factor. It is as big a risk factor as cigarette smoking, obesity, hypertension and low level of physical activity. In one study, it was found that people with the fewest social connections had almost two and a half times as much chance of dying as those with most connections.[6]

People who are socially isolated are more stressed and have fewer outlets for their frustration and lack support. This leads to chronic stress and activation of the stress response, which leads to immune suppression and finally more infectious diseases. Obviously, there are a few other explanations for this phenomenon too. For example, lonely people may not have loved ones asking them to be careful and to look after their health. Simple things like eating out more instead of their home may lead to poor health and higher incidence of disease. Turning the question around—is it the case that sickly people tend to be socially isolated? These are valid counterpoints and help to explain other ways in which social isolation may bring about immune suppression. Careful studies show that stress is one of the major factors in suppressing the immune system in socially isolated people.

---

[6] Such studies use sophisticated statistical analysis to discount the effects of other variables as age, gender, health status, etc.

One of the extreme forms of social isolation is bereavement and a number of studies have shown that the death of a spouse leads to poorer health in the survivor and that there is a higher incidence of death. Popular fiction and movies have used this theme of the grieving spouse pining away for the dead partner and eventually dying.

9.6 Marital Stress

A slew of new research during the past few years shows that marital stress can play a significant role in a person's overall health—increasing risk for everything from chronic pain to a heart attack. A low-stress marriage can even increase survival chances when a health problem strikes. People who are married tend to be healthier and live longer than unmarried people. Scientists are increasingly turning their attention to the quality of marriage. Some of the resulting studies have shown that the risk of a bad marriage is as strong as any other medical risk. Among patients who suffered congestive heart failure, those with good marriages were more likely to survive. One study linked marital distress to dangerous thickening of the heart wall, just like smoking.

Stress is a major risk factor for many health problems but marital stress appears to be a bigger hazard than other types of stress simply because it's so personal. You can't escape marital stress the way you can other types of stress. Most people think of marriage as a comfort zone and a place where you can relax, but when that is stressed, there is no safe haven. The problem is that many people aren't aware how much their marriage is affecting stress levels. Studies have shown that arguments in couples who have been married for decades can increase stress-response hormones that weaken the immune system. As we have seen in the previous chapters, research has linked stress-response hormones to a number of health problems, making a person more susceptible to illness, slowing wound-healing and even interfering with the effectiveness of a vaccine. The most surprising research has focused on a group of newlyweds, who, by all accounts, seemed happy, even 'blissful' in their relationships. But Ohio State University researchers asked the couples to answer questions about their marriage, videotaped them discussing a stressful topic and took blood samples to measure hormones known to inhibit or enhance the immune system. The couples that appeared to become the most agitated and hostile in the videotapes were more likely to see increases in stress-response hormones. Levels of an immune-boosting hormone also dropped. Years later, researchers found the couples who eventually divorced had shown significant elevation in three of four immune-weakening hormones. Since those changes were detected in newlyweds, the research shows that not only did the hormones predict divorce risk, but the study also showed that marital stress, long before it's obvious, can have a measurable impact on the immune system. The same researchers are now studying the role of marital stress on wound healing. The researchers are inflicting small pea-sized blisters on the arms of each spouse, studying whether positive interaction with each other can lead to faster healing by lowering the stress-response hormone. Marriage stress is unique because it takes what should be a person's primary source of support and makes it a primary stressor.

The Harvard Men's Health Watch newsletter examined the relationship between marital stress and heart health, highlighting a study of patients who answered questions on the Dyadic Adjustment Scale (a widely used test used to assess marital stress). The study showed that marital stress was linked with a thickening of the left ventricle of the heart, as seen on an echocardiogram, just like smoking and excessive drinking. But job stress didn't have the same effect. How much you interact with your spouse in a good or bad marriage can also influence your health. The same study found that among people in unhappy marriages, those who spent less time with a spouse had lower blood pressure than those who had lots of contact. Among those in good marriages, people who spent a lot of time with their spouse had even lower blood pressure. It is possible to measure the physiological effect of a stressful interpersonal relationship. But while it's clear that a bad marriage can drastically increase stress, it's not yet known whether it's better, in terms of overall health, to try to improve a troubled relationship or to get a divorce—which itself is an extremely stressful life event.

Even in good marriages, the way a couple interacts appears to affect the health. A Yale study asked couples married for about 40 years to name their confidante or greatest source of emotional support. Surprisingly, a couple in which a woman with children named her husband but the husband didn't name her was significantly more likely to be alive after six years than other couples. One possible explanation may be that being needed, by either your children or your wife, is better for health than having someone to lean on.

9.7 Symptoms of an Infection

In this section we will make a small detour from our general discussion on the topic of stress and the suppression of the immune system. Here, we will examine one particular aspect of the immune system with which we are all so familiar that we tend not to give it any thought—I am talking about the symptoms of feeling sick. Typically, when we get an infection, we have a fever, our joints and muscles hurt, we feel sleepy, lose our appetite and are generally lethargic. These symptoms are so common that usually, we use them to identify when we are sick. The symptoms occur with any other symptoms that may be particular to the specific infection but this basic set does not change. One wonders why different infectious organisms lead to so many common symptoms in humans? The surprising answer is that it is not the infectious organism causing the symptoms but our body that is producing them! For the rest of the story read on...

In an earlier section, we saw how the macrophages identify an infectious agent and raise the metaphorical alarm using the messengers interleukin-1 and -2. It turns out that the messengers are no ordinary carriers but have a surprising array of effects.

9.8 The Influential Messengers

The first part of this story starts in the brain and specifically the hippocampus, which is involved in temperature regulation. In common terms, the hippocampus is the thermostat of the body. Normally, it is set to 98.6°F. It turns out that the hippocampus has a large number of interleukin receptors. What this means is that the hippocampus can sense the levels of interleukin in the blood. The interleukin binds to the receptors in the hippocampus and causes the temperature to be set higher.[7] We begin to feel cold, and muscles start shivering to generate heat. Blood is diverted from the periphery to the internal organs and you start feeling cold—time to pile on the blankets and bring out the sweater. Just to give an idea of the energy involved in this process, in case of malarial fever, the body consumes almost 50 per cent more energy than usual.

There are nerve pathways coming from all over the body to the spinal cord (and then to the brain) that carry pain signals. These pathways have a certain threshold that has to be crossed before the signal is accepted as painful by the brain. A simple congratulatory pat on the back does not cross this threshold and is not painful whereas a sharp blow to the back will definitely be registered as painful. Interleukin-1 does something quite insidious. It lowers the threshold for the pain signal. Suddenly, all the old aches and pains seem to

---

[7] There are several steps between the binding and the rise in temperature. Specifically, after binding to the neurons, it triggers the synthesis of prostaglandins. These chemicals act as signals inside the cells to increase the temperature and increase the pain sensitivity. As an interesting aside, aspirin interferes with the synthesis of the prostaglandin and in turn helps reduce the fever and the pain.

come back. What the body was ignoring is now sending these pain signals and we have aching joints and muscles.

Interleukin also causes the release of a hormone—corticotropin releasing factor (CRF). This is the hormone that initiates the body's stress response and causes the release of other stress-response hormones. Soon, the symptoms associated with stress start to appear. Loss of appetite, lack of interest in sex and energy storage is blocked. If the infection continues for a long time, sperm production declines in males and females may have irregular periods or may stop ovulating altogether.

That is an impressive list of effects for a mere messenger. It seems that these are not mere side effects of some action but the body has evolved these responses and it works hard to bring about these effects. From an evolutionary point of view, it makes sense for the body to bring about symptoms like muscle pain. A sick animal is not fit to go out in the wild looking for food—it is likely to be eaten in no time. Painful joints and muscles and lack of appetite will help in making it rest. This is only a sketchy explanation and does not cover some obvious exceptions like lions and other carnivores without any known predators. Yet, these carnivores show the same response to fighting infections as humans or other animals.

9.9 Why Do We Get a Fever?

The explanation for the fever producing effect is on much stronger ground. Studies have shown that the immune system works more efficiently at higher temperatures—specifically the proliferation of the fighter cells is accelerated at higher temperatures. A wide variety of viruses and bacteria thrive at temperatures below 98.6°. As the body temperature rises, their doubling time slows and in some cases stops altogether. So, it makes sense to have a fever when the body is fighting an infection. In some animal experiments, scientists have found that blocking a fever in an infected animal makes it less likely to survive the infection. These studies need to be corroborated by more research but if proven it will be a surprising twist to the accepted wisdom of treating the fever with medicines like aspirin.

One other point of interest is the use of these interleukins in the treatment of various diseases like cancer. They cause the body's immune system to be activated but they have the nasty side effect of making you feel stupendously sick—something reported by cancer patients treated with interleukin-2.[8]

---

[8] A close relative of interleukin-1.

Chapter 10 | Depression

Depression is like a thick, dark fog. There are several factors that can bring it on: Negative life events such as divorce or cumulative stressors; biological changes, as is the case with post-partum depression and bipolar illness; or by the presence of dysfunctional beliefs such as 'I'm unlovable'. Though depression has various triggers, once it is activated the symptoms are akin regardless of the cause. What is particularly insidious about depression is that when the symptoms are allowed to cycle automatically, the state can maintain itself for weeks, even months.

For simplicity, depression is broken down into its symptom categories so that the tangible aspects can be identified. There are four general symptom areas of depression (see Figure 10.1).

Depressive symptoms feed one another, and this is what prolongs the state. Consider the example of an applicant who is turned down after a job interview and comes to the following conclusions: 'I'm a loser, I'm unemployable'. These self-statements will certainly make her feel sad and guilty (emotional) which, in turn, will lead to a lethargic, listless physical state (physical), to which she might elect to spend all day in bed (behavioural), leading to insomnia that night (physical).

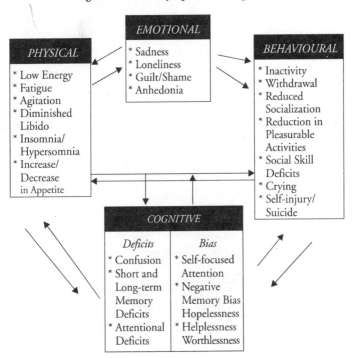

Figure 10.1: The Symptoms of Depression

EMOTIONAL
* Sadness
* Loneliness
* Guilt/Shame
* Anhedonia

PHYSICAL
* Low Energy
* Fatigue
* Agitation
* Diminished Libido
* Insomnia/ Hypersomnia
* Increase/ Decrease in Appetite

BEHAVIOURAL
* Inactivity
* Withdrawal
* Reduced Socialization
* Reduction in Pleasurable Activities
* Social Skill Deficits
* Crying
* Self-injury/ Suicide

COGNITIVE

Deficits
* Confusion
* Short and Long-term Memory Deficits
* Attentional Deficits

Bias
* Self-focused Attention
* Negative Memory Bias Hopelessness
* Helplessness Worthlessness

During the wakeful hours of darkness and silence, she has other thoughts like 'I can't do anything with my life' (cognitive) and to conjure ugly memories of past failures (cognitive). She will undoubtedly have decreased energy the next day (physical) and find it hard to concentrate (cognitive). She may elect to cancel her lunch date with her friend (behavioural) and then think thoughts like 'my whole life is falling apart' (cognitive). This, in turn, will add anxiety to her experience (emotional) which will add restlessness to her fatigue (physical), which may lead to the decision to cancel another scheduled job interview the following day (behavioural) and so on...

Consider the downward spiral depicted in Figure 10.2:

Figure 10.2: Depressive Spiral

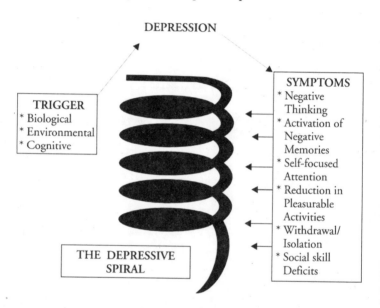

The figure emphasizes the fact that symptoms of depression are not just by-products, but actually serve to strengthen and prolong the depressive state. This may seem like a very discouraging model, but it also offers the logical conclusion that if depressive symptoms perpetuate depression, the reduction of these symptoms would weaken the state. This is exactly what research has shown. Though depression is a self-fuelling state, the cognitive and behavioural symptoms that worsen the state are tangible, and when modified, weaken it.

Like the proverbial story of the blind men trying to describe an elephant by touching one part of the animal, we will try to define depression and its causes by considering the various aspects of the disease:

- The neurochemistry of depression;
- Neuroanatomy of depression;
- Cognitive model of depression.

10.1 The Neurochemistry of Depression

Considerable evidence exists that something is askew with the chemistry of the brains of depressives. In order to appreciate that, it is necessary to understand a little about how brain cells communicate with one another. The basic structural and functional unit of the nervous system is the nerve cell or neuron, which is the principal type of brain cell. The neurons are similar to other cells in the body except for two projections—antenna like structures called dendrites for receiving signals and a long projection for transmitting signals called axon. An axon is capable of transmitting a pulse of electricity (nerve impulse) from the neuron body to some distant target in the brain or the periphery. However, two neurons do not communicate with electrical signals. In fact, there is a small gap between the end of the axon of one neuron and the dendrite of the next neuron (the scientific term for this gap is synapse). The electrical impulse does not cross this gap, but rather causes a chemical (neurotransmitter) to be released from the axon terminals. The neurotransmitter diffuses across the gap and causes electrical changes to occur in the second cell.

Say, a neuron has become excited with some thought or memory (metaphorically speaking); the excitement is an electrical signal—a wave of electricity sweeps from the dendrites over the neuron body, down the axon to the axon terminals. When the wave of electrical excitation reaches the axon terminal, it releases chemical messengers across the synapse. These messengers called 'neurotransmitters' bind to specialized receptors on the adjacent dendrite causing the second neuron to be electrically excited.

A small but important piece of housekeeping—what happens to the neurotransmitter after it has done its job and floats off the receptor? In some cases it is recycled—that is taken up by the axon of the first neuron and repackaged for future use. Alternatively, it can be degraded in the synapse and the debris flushed out to the cerebrospinal fluid, then to the blood and the urine. If these processes fail—either the reuptake by the axon or the degradation in the synapse, then suddenly a lot more neurotransmitter remains in the synapse giving a stronger signal to the second neuron. The proper disposal of the neurotransmitter is a critical piece of neuronal communication.

There are billions of synapses in the brain but only a few hundred neurotransmitters. The same neurotransmitters convey different messages in different parts of the brain. Say, at one synapse, neurotransmitter A sends a message relevant to pancreatic regulation while at another synapse the same neurotransmitter may pertain to emotion.

The best neurochemical evidence suggests that depression involves abnormal levels of one or both of a pair of neurotransmitters—norepinephrine and serotonin. Most of the drugs that lessen depression increase the amount of signalling by these neurotransmitters. One class of anti-depressant called tricyclics, stops the recycling or reuptake of norepinephrine and serotonin in the axon terminals. The result is that the neurotransmitters remain in the synapse longer and is likely to bind to the receptors a second or third time.

A second class of drugs called MAO inhibitors, blocks the degradation of norepinephrine and serotonin in the synapse by inhibiting the action of a crucial enzyme in the degradation, monoamine oxidase (MAO). The result is that more of the messengers remain in the synapses. These findings generate a pretty straightforward conclusion—if you use a drug that increases the amount of norepinephrine and serotonin in the synapses throughout the brain, and as a result someone's depression gets better, there must have been too little of those neurotransmitters in the first place. Is the case closed? Naturally, anything connected with the brain is not that simple. As a first issue of confusion, is the problem in depression too little of serotonin or norepinephrine or both? As the tricyclics and MAO inhibitors work on both, it is impossible to say. A class of drugs called SSRI (selective serotonin reuptake inhibitors) work only on serotonin synapses and they work for a large number of patients. A newer class of drugs targets either or both the neurotransmitters depending on drug dosage and have also proven to be very effective.

Another question is whether the real problem is too little of the neurotransmitter in the first place? The stumbling block has to do with timing. In a laboratory, expose the brain to tricyclics and signalling in the synapses changes within hours. However, give that same drug to a depressed person, and it takes weeks for the person to feel better.

There are two main theories that attempt to explain this timing problem and both are fairly complicated as they try to make sense of this rather anomalous result. I will provide a simplified explanation below.

10.2 Neurochemical Theory 1 of Depression

'It is not too little but actually too much norepinephrine'. First, some background orientation. If somebody constantly yells or shouts at you, you stop listening. Similarly, if you surround a cell with lots of a neurotransmitter, the cell will not 'listen' as carefully—in scientific terms the cell will down regulate (decrease) the number of receptors for that neurotransmitter, in order to decrease its sensitivity to that messenger. For example, if you double the amount of serotonin reaching the dendrites of a cell and that cell downgrades its serotonin receptors by 50 per cent, the effects roughly cancel out. If it down regulates by less than 50 per cent, the result will be more signalling and if it down regulates by more than 50 per cent, there will be less serotonin signalling in the synapse. In other words, how strong the signal is depends on how loudly the first neuron is shouting (amount of neurotransmitter being released) and how sensitively the second neuron listens. The theory states that in patients with depression, there is too much norepinephrine, serotonin or both in parts of the brain. What happens if you prescribe medicines that increase these neurotransmitters even more? At first, the symptoms should get worse (this happens in a number of patients). Over the course of a few weeks the dendrites say, 'there is too much shouting—I cannot bear it. Let us down regulate our receptors a whole lot'. If this down regulation compensates for the extra signalling, the effects of excessive neurotransmitter will go and the person starts to feel better.

10.3 Neurochemical Theory 2 of Depression

'The problem with depressive patients is too little of norepinephrine or serotonin or both'. Remember our discussion on neuron communication—at that time, we said the transmitting neuron has receptors for absorbing some of the neurotransmitter it has released. This process known as 'reuptake' is critical for proper neuronal communication. Why does the transmitting neuron reuptake the neurotransmitter? One reason is to decide on how much neurotransmitter to release or whether to stop releasing the neurotransmitter. With this as a background, we will now try to understand the theory. Give a patient anti-depressant drugs that increase the levels of neurotransmitters. Due to the increased signalling, there will be down-regulation of the receptors over a period of weeks. The main argument is the idea that the autoreceptor on the transmitting neuron will down regulate more than the receptor on the second (listening) neuron. If this is the case, the second neuron may not be listening effectively, but the first neuron will be sending out a lot more neurotransmitter. The net result is enhanced levels of serotonin or norepinephrine and the patient feels better. For a long time, psychiatrists have used this technique to alleviate major depression using ECT (electro convulsive therapy also known as 'shock' treatment). In animal experimentation, it has been observed that ECT decreases the number of norepinephrine autoreceptors.

At this point in time, there is considerable research and debate going on to explain the neurochemistry of depression. The best treatment for depressives seems to be newer drugs that target both serotonin and norepinephrine depending on the dosage and the symptoms. It is also important to note that there are several other neurotransmitters implicated in depression though their role is not as clear. Recall that one of the key signs of depression is lack of 'pleasure' or anhedonia. It is logical to assume that the portions of the brain involved with feelings of pleasure or sadness must have something to do with depression. In fact, there is such a region in the brain and a neurotransmitter named dopamine[1] which is involved in feelings of pleasure. Some researchers have implicated problems with dopamine levels in cases of depression. However, these are tentative findings and more research needs to be done before the details are sorted out.

One of the key factors in depression is the role of psychological stress. Repeated studies have demonstrated a clear

---

[1] Cocaine and other drugs bind to the dopamine receptors and produce the intense 'high' or euphoria reported by drug addicts.

link between stress and the onset of depression. The body's stress response is thought to be the main cause of disruption in the levels of neurotransmitters. A very important caveat— studies have shown that the first few episodes of depression are preceded by stressful events but after that depression takes on a cycle of its own and is no longer related to stress.

Another important point to note is that more women suffer from depression than men (ratio is almost 2 to 1). Usually, these episodes occur at times when a woman's body undergoes changes in hormone levels—puberty, menstruation, pregnancy/delivery and menopause. A number of researchers believe such increased risks for women are tied to the great fluctuations that occur during menstruation, menopause and parturition in the two main hormones—estrogen and progesterone. As evidence, they cite the fact that women can get depressed when they artificially change their estrogen or progesterone levels (for example, when taking birth control pills). Critically, both these hormones can regulate neurochemical events in the brain—including the metabolism of neurotransmitters such as norepinephrine and serotonin. This is a new area of research with some seemingly contradictory findings, but there is increased confidence among scientists that there is a hormonal contribution to the preponderance of female depressions.

10.4 Neuroanatomy of Depression

The top layer of the brain is the cortex—the area involved in abstract thinking, cognition, philosophical thought and memory functions. This portion is extremely large and well developed in primates as compared to other animals.

Just below the cortex is the limbic system. This area is associated with emotions and response to stress. At an incredibly simplistic level, we can think of depression as a condition where the cortex thinks of some sad thoughts and convinces the rest of the brain that it is real. It is as if in depressives, the cortex continuously whispers sad thoughts to the rest of the brain. The veracity of this model of depression is proved by a very crude surgical technique. Cut off the connections between the cortex and rest of the brain and the depression should go away. This crude technique actually works and it is called a cingulotomy. Obviously, this treatment is rarely, if ever, practiced.

10.5 Stress and the Onset of Depression

The first stress-depression link is an obvious one. Statistically, stress and the onset of depression go together. People who are undergoing a lot of life stressors are more likely to succumb to depression and people in depression are more likely to have undergone a recent significant stressor.

Laboratory studies also link stress and the symptoms of depression. Stress a lab rat and it becomes anhedonic—specifically, the threshold for perceiving pleasure has been raised, just as in a person suffering from depression.

The body's hormonal response to stress (particularly the glucocorticoids hormones) affects the neurotransmitters and their metabolism. Specifically, glucocorticoids cause a change in the amounts of neurotransmitters synthesized, how fast it is broken down, how many receptors are there for each neurotransmitter, how well the receptors work and so on.

10.6 Cognitive Model of Depression

The field of experimental psychology provides some excellent theoretical understanding about stress and depression. The key point from this theory is that events are considered psychologically stressful when they have some of the following characteristics—a loss of control and predictability within certain contexts, a loss of outlets for frustration, a loss of source of support, a perception that in some aspects life is getting worse. In a number of experiments, when animals are subjected to stressful events that have these characteristics, the result is a condition similar to human depression. While the actual stressors may differ, the general approach in these studies always emphasizes repeated stressors with a complete absence of control on the part of the animal (for example in humans, people who have close friends or relatives who suffer from incurable diseases and are dying. The feeling of helplessness is most acute in such instances). After a while under such circumstances, the animal has trouble coping with day-to-day tasks. This phenomenon is called 'learned helplessness'. This is similar to the depressed person who does not even try to perform the simplest task. Animals with learned helplessness also have a cognitive problem, something awry with how they perceive the world and think about it.

To summarize, stress, particularly in the form of extremes of lack of control and outlets, causes an array of deleterious changes in a person—

- Cognitively, this involves a distortive belief that there is no control or outlets in any circumstances—learned helplessness.
- On the affective level, there is anhedonia—the threshold for pleasure is very high.
- Behaviourally, there is psychomotor retardation.
- On the neurochemical front, there are likely disruptions of serotonin, norepinephrine and dopamine signalling.
- Physiologically, there are alterations in appetite, sleep patterns, pain perception, and sensitivity of the glucocorticoids feedback system.

Collectively all these array of changes are called depression. One key question about the stress-depression link is not fully answered: why is it that the stress-depression link uncouples after three or four bouts of depression? Remember our earlier discussion about depressive episodes taking on an internal rhythm of their own, independent of whether the outside world is pummelling you with stressors. There are a lot of theories that attempt to provide explanations but there is very little by way of actual data.

10.7 Depression in Women

Earlier in the chapter we had touched upon some of the causes of the higher rates of depression in women. Here, we will explore the topic in more detail. For centuries, doctors have recognized women's vulnerability to depression and proposed a variety of explanations. At the beginning of the century, the female of the species, with her 'excitable nervous system,' was thought to wilt under the strain of menstruation and childbirth, or later, the pressures of work and family. But researchers are now constructing more scientific theories to explain why women are nearly twice as likely as men to become depressed. Experts say that social bias and women's higher rates of physical and sexual abuse and poverty play a role in this. But scientists are also studying genes that may predispose girls and women to the disorder. They are examining the likely role of estrogen and even linking the development of clinical depression to negative thinking, which is more common in women than in men.

There is no question that women bear the brunt of depression. The National Co-morbidity Study, a large survey of adults in the US released in 2003, found that almost two women for every man had experienced at least one episode of depression. Roughly the same ratio has been found in recent studies in nine other countries including Canada, Brazil, Germany and Japan.

It is unlikely that any single gene, hormone level or type of experience explains the higher incidence of depression in women. Instead, several genes probably work in concert with the ebb and flow of reproductive hormones to change brain chemistry in ways that might set the stage for depression, especially after an emotional ordeal. Another risk factor appears to be something that researchers call 'over-thinking', a tendency to dwell on petty slights, to mentally replay testy encounters and to wallow in sad feelings. Studies show that this type of negative thinking is far more common in women than in men, and that it can be a harbinger of clinical depression.

Experts feel that the gender difference in over-thinking is strongly tied to the gender difference in depression.

About half the risk of depression is thought to be genetic. The single gene, 5-HTT, that has been definitively linked to depression is no more common in women than in men. But preliminary research suggests that there are other depression-related genes that mainly affect women. For example, after scanning the genomes of people with major depression in families, scientists have identified 19 regions of chromosomes that were especially common and, therefore, likely to contain genes that promote depression. Four of these regions showed up only in women and one in men. Such findings suggest that more genes may help to set off depression in women than in men, explaining in part why more women become depressed. One may be CREB1, a gene that has recently been identified as a strong candidate. Especially intriguing, is the fact that CREB1 interacts with estrogen receptors.

Though the details of the relationship between CREB1 and estrogen are unknown, researchers have long thought that levels of sex hormones play some role in depression. For one thing, sex difference in depression is most pronounced in women during their reproductive years, when sex hormone levels are highest. Before puberty, boys and girls have roughly equal rates of depression. The incidence of depression climbs in both sexes during puberty, but the climb is steepest for girls. In a national telephone survey in the US of 12 to 17 year-olds, about 14 per cent of girls and 7 per cent of boys met the criteria for major depression. In their reproductive years, women are also especially prone to bouts of depression when their sex hormones are in flux—just before menstruation and just after childbirth. Two sub-types of depression that affect only women—premenstrual disorder and postpartum depression—occur at these times.

A leading theory is that sex hormones help induce depression in some women by affecting neurotransmitters in the brain that influence mood. The sensitivity of these neurotransmitters may increase when hormone levels are high or in a state of flux and decrease when they are low and stable. However, to blame women's higher rate of depression on hormones is too simplistic, say experts. Not all women become depressed when their hormone levels seesaw.

A study sponsored by the National Institute of Mental Health in the US showed that manipulating women's levels of estrogen and progesterone affected the moods of some women but not others. Specifically, women who usually suffered from premenstrual syndrome, a condition characterized by moodiness in the week or so before menstruation that is less severe than premenstrual disorder, found that their moods lifted when they were given a drug that kept their hormone levels low. When their hormone levels went back to normal, these women felt blue. But women who did not suffer from premenstrual syndrome did not experience ups and downs in mood during the study. Such findings indicate that it is not hormone levels per se that make some women feel moody or depressed at times of hormonal flux, but an underlying vulnerability. The big question is 'What is that vulnerability?'

Current research indicates that genes may tell much of this story. Some genes that raise women's risk of depression may exert their effect in the presence of high levels of estrogen, their influence then decreasing when estrogen falls after menopause. But biology cannot entirely explain the sex difference.

Another important factor is the greater tendency of girls and women to ruminate over the common problems of life like criticism at work or school or rejection by a friend. In several studies over the last decade, scientists have found that women react more strongly than men to such experiences, mulling over them without being able to come to a resolution or to simply move on. Dwelling on problems causes the initial sadness to snowball. In contrast, men are more likely to distract themselves from a problem, often by doing some physical activity, and this helps to blunt the emotional sting of everyday disappointments and setbacks. Some studies have found that people who habitually ruminate but are not depressed are more likely than non-ruminators to develop depression later.

There may be biological reasons behind women's tendency to brood, but no genetic predisposition or difference in the brain has been found. In all likelihood, there are cultural and personality contributors to rumination. Women tend to forge intense emotional connections and to care deeply about relationships. Such an investment in relationships can be a source of great richness in women's lives, but taken too far, it can also become destructive. A few studies have found that sex difference in negative thinking is apparent in children as young as nine, several years earlier than the sex difference in depression emerges.

Several strategies can be employed—staying active can help. For teenage girls, playing a sport or engaging in other extra-curricular activities can keep them from brooding about bad marks in exams or broken romances. If their self-esteem hinges on one thing, like a single relationship, there is no fallback if something goes wrong. Another strategy is to cultivate a circle of friends. When women ruminate, they tend to blow things up. It helps to have friends who can help you reflect on a problem and find a solution. On a lighter note, it is important to make sure that the friends are not too prone to rumination themselves.

10.8 Pepsi vs Coke

In this chapter, we have looked at the way in which the brain affects our mood and how psychological stress is the trigger for depression. We will now look at another instance where the brain influences what we sense.

When he isn't pondering the inner workings of the mind, Read Montague, a neuroscientist at Baylor College of Medicine, has been known to contemplate the other mysteries of life: for instance, the Pepsi Challenge. In a series of TV commercials in the US from the 1970s and 1980s that pitted Coke against Pepsi in a blind taste test, Pepsi was usually the winner. So why, Montague asked himself not long ago, did Coke appeal so strongly to so many people if it didn't taste any better?

Montague set to work looking for a scientifically convincing answer. He assembled a group of test subjects and, while monitoring their brain activity with an MRI machine, recreated the Pepsi Challenge. His results confirmed those of the TV campaign: Pepsi tended to produce a stronger response than Coke in the brain's ventral putamen, a region thought to process feelings of reward (monkeys, for instance, exhibit activity in the ventral putamen when they receive food for completing a task). Indeed, in people who preferred Pepsi, the ventral putamen was five times as active when drinking Pepsi than that of Coke fans when drinking Coke.

In the real world, of course, taste is not everything. So, Montague tried to gauge the appeal of Coke's image, its 'brand influence,' by repeating the experiment with a small variation: this time, he announced which of the sample tastes were Coke. The outcome was remarkable: almost all the subjects said they preferred Coke. What's more, the brain activity of the subjects was now different. There was also activity in the pre-frontal cortex; an area of the brain that scientists say governs high-level cognitive powers. Apparently, the subjects were meditating in a more sophisticated way on the taste of Coke, allowing memories and other impressions of the drink—in a word, its brand—to shape their preference.

Pepsi, crucially, couldn't achieve the same effect. When Montague reversed the situation, announcing which tastes were of Pepsi, far fewer of the subjects said they preferred it. Montague was impressed: he had demonstrated, with a fair degree of scientific precision, the special power of Coke's brand to override our taste buds.

The frontal cortex region of the brain is commonly associated with our sense of self. Patients with damage in this area of the brain often undergo drastic changes in personality; in one famous case, a mild-mannered 19th-century rail worker named Phineas Gage abruptly became belligerent after an accident that destroyed his medial pre-frontal cortex. More recently, MRI studies have found increased activity in this region when people are asked if adjectives like 'trustworthy' or 'courageous' apply to them. When the pre-frontal cortex fires, your brain seems to be engaging, in some manner, with what sort of a person you are. For the readers interested in religion and metaphysics, the cortex is the nearest anatomical equivalent of a 'super ego'.

Alert readers may remember our discussion about repressive personalities in chapter 7 and on the role played by the frontal cortex in the brains of repressives. I give this interesting aside on the power of brands to bring home the point about the way in which our perceptions of things can influence our actions and our senses. One point is in order here—many scientists are sceptical of the use of neurology in marketing. The brain, they point out, is still an enigma; just because we can see neurons firing doesn't mean we always know what the mind is doing.

Chapter 11	Memory and Stress	

Stress—Friend or Foe?

A little sharpens the mind and memory; too much shrivels the brain and makes you sick.

The quote above captures the essence of the effects of stress on memory. In the following sections, we will examine in greater detail how the memory system functions and see exactly how stress disrupts the different functions.

11.1 Human Memory

The Ebbinghaus experiment almost 150 years ago was the first real experiment on memory, in particular the remembering of trigrams (for example, DAX, LOC). All these had no meaning but were all distinct monosyllabic words. He measured the retention that he himself had of the words by counting the number of re-learns required to achieve perfect recall and recite them correctly. His results show that retention decreases over time, but the rate of forgetting slows down. He also looked at the effects of over learning and found that through over learning a higher score can be reached on his retention test.

Scientists do not yet understand many things about human memory and many of the ideas and theories are still quite controversial. The following discussion emphasizes some of the more widely agreed upon ideas. For instance, most scientists agree that it is very useful to describe human memory as a set of stores, which are 'places' to put information, plus a set of processes that act on the stores.

A very simple model might contain three different stores:

- The Sensory Information Store (SIS);
- The Short-term Store (STS);
- The Long-term Store (LTS).

and three processes:

- Encoding (putting information into a store);
- Maintenance (keeping it 'alive');
- Retrieval (finding encoded information).

11.2 Long-term Memory (Store)

Long-term memory (LTM) was once thought of as a huge database where information was simply filed away in the same manner as a filing cabinet. LTM is often studied with normal people to assess its limits and characteristics. In order to determine the neural pathways to LTM, however, we must start with a brain that is damaged and then assess the deficiencies that the individual faces with respect to LTM. This deficiency may arise from an accident, pathology, or in the case of animal models, intentionally inflicted. Today,

LTM in humans is believed to be partitioned into specialized modules:

Long-term Memory

Declarative Memory   Procedural Memory

Diencephalon   Hippocampus   Amygdala   Cerebellum

Research into the neurological basis of long-term memory generally involves studying those individuals who have had their brain structures altered in some way. Since it is considered unethical to knowingly induce brain damage on a human, researchers often use animal models to directly study cause-effect relationships.

With equipment, such as, MRI, CAT, and PET scans, brain damage can be localized with more precision than previously possible. These tests, however, only reveal the biological and pathological nature of the brain trauma and not the functional characteristic of that affected region. In order to determine the function of a damaged region, researchers often have individuals, with a known damage to the brain, perform memory tasks which are thought to require the use of a certain type of long-term memory store. As an example, performance in real-time tracking in a task such as rotary pursuit is seen to improve in individuals who are unable to access other areas of the long-term memory. By determining what the individual can and cannot do with their damaged brain, researchers are able to infer what role a particular area of the brain plays in long-term memory.

11.3 What is Declarative Memory?

Declarative memory is our memory for facts. There is a common belief that declarative memory is further broken down into two components: Episodic (memory for past and personally experienced events), and Semantic (knowledge for the meaning of words and how to apply them).

In general, the hippocampus and cortex are involved in declarative memory. Neocortex is also associated with declarative memory. In particular, this includes the right frontal and temporal lobes for the episodic component, and the temporal lobes for the semantic component.

The psychologist who first proposed this idea was Endel Tulving. In the case of episodic memory, Tulving notes that the subject not only has the memory, but can remember something about the setting in which the memory was learned. Conversely, for semantic memory, the subject cannot recall the context of the initial learning.

Tulving argued that episodic memory was the system that was tested in most memory experiments, which required subjects to recall lists of words. He reasoned that if a subject failed to recall a word in a particular list, it was due to the fact that he/she failed to recall a particular episode (i.e., list) and not the meaning of the word. Semantic memory can be defined as the knowledge for the meaning of words and how to apply them. For example, if we are asked to memorize a list of fruits and then, during a recall, if we fail to remember say mango and apple, it is not because we have forgotten these common names. It is because we fail to remember them as part of the list. This caused Tulving to make the distinction between memory for 'meanings' (semantic) versus memory for 'episodes' or experiences (episodic).

Studies of amnesiacs have been the most common form of evidence used to distinguish declarative memory from the other prominent type of LTM known as procedural memory. Amnesiacs are known to lack the ability to add to their declarative memory stores (episodic or semantic).

A well-known case in medical research involves the patient known as HM, who had the anterior and medial portions of his temporal lobes removed to prevent epileptic seizures. HM and similar patients have normal memory of events before their trauma but they can't form new long-term memories. This suggests that the frontal and medial temporal lobe structures are required for adding information to declarative memory. Several researchers have accepted this case as support for the distinction of memory pathways.

11.4 What is Procedural Memory?

Procedural memory is memory storage of skills and procedures. This type of memory has also been referred to as 'tacit knowledge' or 'implicit knowledge'. Procedural memory is involved in tasks such as remembering how to swim or how to ride a bicycle. This is 'knowhow' memory; it often can only be expressed by performing the specific skill and people have problems verbalizing what they are doing and why. Procedural memory is, therefore, very important in human motor performance.

Procedural memory has been broken down into three separate groups: conditioned reflexes, emotional associations, and skills and habits. Each of these memories is associated with probable anatomical structures in the brain. Memories and learning of conditioned reflexes such as pulling your hand away from a hot fire is related to the cerebellum. On the other hand, emotional associations such as knowing when to be afraid or mad in a particular situation are related to the amygdala.

11.5 How is Memory Stored?

We now turn to the important question of how memory is actually stored. As you can expect, there are a number of theories that attempt to explain this. Early work had suggested that there were brain cells that stored specific information. For example, there may be brain cells that store information about faces or some that store information about paintings and so on. Obviously, there is too much information to be stored in this way. A logical way to store information would be to organize it as a pattern and store that pattern in a network of brain cells. The advantage of storing information in networks as opposed to discrete chunks is that memory will not be totally lost. It will be accessible through different routes. Typically, when we are trying to remember a name or a date, we try and use associated information—things like 'I know it rhymes with car' or, 'It was a company party when I had met him' and so on. These associations help us in recalling many facts. The common term used for such a network is 'Neural Network'. It is interesting to note that this term has entered popular literature due to its use in computer science. Some years back, modelling human memory and developing programmes to mimic the human model of learning were a rage in computer science research and the term neural network entered the popular lexicon.

I will give a very simple description of how a neural network works in storing information. Consider a network of neurons that are interconnected. At the bottom of the network are the neurons that store one simple fact. Say, each neuron at the bottom knows one car model. The neuron at the next level has connections to all the other neurons. At the lowest level, one of the neurons knows about a Maruti Zen while its neighbour may know about an Indica. The next step up knows about different medium-sized cars and knows about 'B-segment or mid-sized' cars. It has knowledge that does not come from any single input, but emerges from the convergence of information feeding into it. The next level up may know about cars from different countries and may be associated with information about those countries and so on. We take advantage of such linked information when trying to recall a particular piece of information.

The above is a wildly simplistic explanation of how memory is organized. As you can imagine, there are no specialized neurons that know about cars or other facts for that matter. Neuroscientists think of learning and storing of information as a process that strengthens some part of a neural network.

The obvious question to ask is how does such strengthening take place? Recall from our discussion on neural communication in chapter 10 on depression, that neurons communicate with each other using neurotransmitters. The neurotransmitters with a role in depression that we looked at were serotonin and norepinephrine. The stores of long-term memory use the neurotransmitter glutamate. This is a very excitable transmitter and the neurons that are sensitive to this transmitter have two very important properties:

- The synapses are non-linear in their function. To understand this concept better, let us take the case of two neurons communicating using glutamate. The first neuron has some exciting information (metaphorically speaking) to pass on to the second neuron. It sends out some glutamate. Nothing happens. It sends out some more glutamate and still nothing happens. It is only when the glutamate passes some threshold that the second neuron receives it and gets all excited. Many of us have had this experience when learning some new or complicated subject. We read about it 20 times and it is all a big mystery. Somewhere around the 21st time, we have that 'Aha!' moment and it becomes clear. On a simplistic level, it can be said that the threshold for excitation has been passed.

- After a certain number of excitations, the synapse becomes persistently more excitable. Say, a neuron has been excited repeatedly by the glutamate. At some point, the neuron becomes super sensitive to the glutamate. Now, even a smidgen of the glutamate can get the neuron all excited. This is the stage when we say that the neuron has just 'learned' something. The scientific term for this phenomenon is 'potentiation'. The important thing to note is that this potentiation can last for a very long time.

11.6 Effects of Stress on Memory

At the beginning of this chapter, we mentioned that little stress sharpens the memory. The explanation for this from the evolutionary point of view is really simple. Faced with a predator, it makes sense for you to remember all the things you did previously that saved your life. It also helps to memorize hiding places, special dangers and all other information that will help you escape the predator in future. There are two ways in which the memory is improved during short stressors. First, as blood flow increases with the onset of a stressor, more energy is available to the brain and that helps in improving the performance of the neurons. The potentiation of neurons[1] is an expensive operation and the extra energy helps in that process. The second way is through the

---

[1] It is amazing to note how expensive thinking is (in terms of energy requirements). The brain accounts for only 3 per cent of our body weight but hogs about 20 per cent of the energy.

effects of the glucocorticoids on the hippocampus in a localized effect. The hippocampus has numerous receptors for the glucocorticoids and they reduce the threshold for potentiation—the number of 'Ahas!' required for the neuron to learn something.

When the stress goes on for too long, bad things start to happen. Instead of helping the potentiation, the glucocorticoids now disrupt it. Worse, there can be memory loss in a process called long-term depression. The mechanism for this process is not clear but the effect is obvious—you start to forget things easily. Further, the glucose delivery (energy) is disrupted. The neurons in the hippocampus now take up 25 per cent less energy and the result is that your memory and concentration suffer. With chronic stress, something truly insidious begins to happen—the neurons get damaged. The branches of the neural network are retracted. It is not that the memory is lost—we just need more associations to retrieve it. There is some research in animals that shows that prolonged exposure to glucocorticoids kills neurons in the hippocampus. This has not been proven in humans but it clearly indicates the dangerous possibilities.

11.7 Alzheimer's Disease and Stress

People who get more upset by disturbing events are more likely to suffer the declines in memory and mental ability found in Alzheimer's disease, according to a study published recently. The study tracked a group of priests, nuns and monks as part of a long-term examination of the aging process.

According to Dr Robert S. Wilson of the Rush Alzheimer's Disease Center in Chicago (the study's lead author), earlier research had shown that chronic stress undermined the functioning of the part of the brain governing memory. He and his colleagues wondered if a lifetime of stress could make people more vulnerable to Alzheimer's. They tested the idea on members of the Religious Orders Study, whose life experiences were more similar than the general population's. There were 800 members, with an average age of 75, who completed surveys in an effort to gauge what researchers called 'distress proneness', that is how likely reactions to stress would result in gloom or anxiety, a trait also known as neuroticism. Various memory and other mental tasks were also measured. The subjects were re-examined five years later. In the meantime, Alzheimer's had been diagnosed in 140 of them. People who had scored the highest on the neuroticism test were twice as likely to have developed the condition as those who scored the lowest. Dr Rush describes the low scorers as 'secure, hardy and generally relaxed,' even when factors like depression were accounted for. Even among those who had not developed Alzheimer's, higher scores on the test were associated with faster rates of decline, particularly in memory.

Chapter 12 | Pain

In the last few months of 2003, newspapers in India had been running full-page advertisements from an oil company. The advertisements described the life story and achievements of individuals who succeeded against all odds and inspired others. One life story struck me as particularly poignant. It is the story of a brave captain in the Indian Army. Barely a year and a half out of the Indian Military Academy in Dehra Dun, the young captain and his team is asked to defend the country against terrorists in the inhospitable terrain of Kargil in the Himalayas. There the team of brave soldiers crawls on their bellies while their backs are torn by barbed wire and they face withering gunfire and grenades. As they reach the enemy, the captain's colleague is hurt and falls in a trench near the enemy facing sure death. The captain makes a heroic decision, risks his life and leaps in after his wounded colleague. He is hit by enemy gunfire from all sides and has a bullet hole in his chest. No matter; he goes ahead and wipes out the enemy before laying down his life. He manages to save his partner as well as the lives of his teammates but at the cost of his own life. His colleagues can only speak with awe about his heroic leap. A grateful nation can only offer him its highest award for bravery.[1]

---

[1] The captain's name was Vikram Batra and he was awarded the highest award for bravery—Param Veer Chakra—in recognition of his heroic fight.

Every time I read that advertisement I am saddened at the loss of the young life but am also struck by one remarkable fact. Under extreme stress, the soldiers did not feel the pain while the barbed wire tore their backs. More particularly, the captain continued to fire and attack the enemy even after sustaining gunshot wounds himself. We can only speculate what his thoughts must have been at that time but we can almost be positive that he did not feel the pain of the bullets at that time. The absence of pain under stress is the subject of this chapter and to give it the correct scientific name it is described as stress-induced analgesia. One of the first persons to record this phenomenon was an anesthesiologist Henry Beecher who examined soldiers during World War II. He found that for injuries of a similar severity, approximately 80 per cent of the civilians requested morphine, while only 30 per cent of the soldiers did.

12.1 How Do We Feel Pain?

To understand stress-induced analgesia, it is necessary for us to understand how the body perceives pain and how it responds to the pain signal. Here, we confront an anatomical problem. The sensors for pain are scattered all over the body. The central nervous system (CNS) processes the signals from the sensors. This is housed entirely within the cranial cavity housing the brain, and the vertebral canal, housing the spinal cord. The response to the pain has to be transmitted to the muscles, which also lie at a distance from the brain and the spinal cord. Therefore, there needs to be some way of relaying sensory input and motor outflow between the periphery and the CNS. This is the function of the peripheral nervous system (PNS). So, how do the pain signals travel from the rest of the body to the brain?

An elegant (now very famous) theory about how pain is perceived is called the Gate Control Theory devised by Patrick Wall and Ronald Melzack in 1965. This theory states that pain is a function of the balance between the information travelling into the spinal cord through slow nerve fibres and information travelling into the spinal cord through fast nerve fibres.

I give below a wildly simplified explanation of this theory. The basic idea is that there are two pathways for communicating pain signals to the brain—a fast path and a slow path. There are two gates (let us call them Gate 1 and Gate 2) through which both these pathways pass. When a signal arrives on the fast path, it passes through both gates and then to the brain where the pain is registered. However, after the fast signal has passed, Gate 2 plays a trick and closes down Gate 1. This stops additional pain signals from reaching the brain. So, we feel only a short sharp pain. When a signal arrives on the slow path, both gates are opened and the brain registers the pain. However, the slow fibre is well aware of the trick played by Gate 2 and stops it from closing Gate 1. Both gates remain open and we continue to feel a constant pain.

Now for a quick lesson on how to reduce throbbing pain—say from an aching muscle. What you need to do is briefly stimulate the fast fibre by a short painful stimulus. This will result in the Gate 2 pulling off its neat trick of closing Gate 1 and temporarily stopping the slow pain signal from reaching the brain. Now with this understanding, we know why a good vigorous massage makes our dull pain go away for a while. This is also true in the case of insect bites that throb and itch. A good hard scratch right around the area relieves the pain. In all these cases, the slow pain pathway is shut down temporarily. Naturally, the pain will return after a time if the cause of the pain has not been resolved.

A more advanced use of this same trick is seen in machines called TENS—trans-electrical nerve stimulators. These devices are commonly used by physiotherapists or during labour and they stimulate the sharp pain fibre in peripheral nerves which will in turn shut the slow pain fibre.

12.2 Neurochemistry of Stress-induced Analgesia

With this background, we can understand the story of the neurochemistry of stress-induced analgesia that began in the early 1970s. It was a time of the hippie culture in America and the rest of the world. The young men and women in the West had then discovered the joys of opiates and the pleasures to be derived from them. Naturally, the leading-edge scientists of that time wanted to know how the various drugs like heroin, morphine, and opium worked. All those drugs have a fairly similar chemical structure and are made by plants in the same way. In a surprising scientific race, three groups of scientists almost simultaneously reported that these drugs worked by binding to receptors in the brain. It turns out that these receptors are located in areas where the brain processes pain perception. As these drugs bind to the receptors, they activate the descending projections from the brain that, in turn, blunt the sensitivity of the pain neuron X (what we called Gate 1 in our discussion in the previous section). Net result of the opiates—pain is blocked!

Just as you digest this explanation, a puzzle hits you like a meteor. Why should the brain have receptors for chemicals made by some plants? The obvious answer comes flooding in: there must be similar chemicals made by our body. The body must make some kind of morphine.

The story lurches forward as enthusiastic teams of neurochemists rushed to discover the endogenous opiates. It would be a tremendous achievement to find the body's natural painkillers. Going further, if synthetic versions of these body painkillers could be made without being addictive, fame and fortune would surely follow. In the ensuing decade, competing teams of scientists found exactly what they were looking for—the compounds made by the body (endogenous compounds) with chemical structure closely linked to the plant opiates. Three classes of chemicals were discovered— enkephalins, dynorphins and endorphins (abbreviation for endogenous morphine). The opiate receptors of the brain were found to bind to these endogenous chemicals just as expected. Furthermore, these opiates were synthesized and released in that part of the brain which processes pain. The rest as they say is history.

We all know about the famed *runners high*—that irrational feeling of euphoria and lack of pain that comes at the 30- or 40-minute mark into strenuous exercise. During exercise, beta-endorphin pours out of the pituitary gland. Around the 30-minute mark enough of it builds up in the bloodstream to cause analgesia. Enkephalins are also activated in the brain and spine. They activate the descending pathways to shut out the action of neuron X. All sorts of other stressors produce similar effects. Surgery, childbirth, examinations, and exposure to cold all cause the same analgesia. From an evolutionary point of view, this is another example of a system that works as expected. As an animal experiencing the stress of being chased by a predator or involved in a dominance fight with another member of the family, it makes sense that a system has evolved to suppress the pain. Now would be a wrong time to feel the aching joint or the pain from the sharp claws. So, where is the problem? Fortunately, this is one system where no one has shown any problem from repeated activation. That is one less excuse for couch potatoes for not exercising. Repeated releases of beta-endorphins have no ill-effects and the exercise will do you a lot of good.

Therefore, I urge all the readers to put down this book and do their exercise before continuing! The only bad news in the release of the body's opiates is that it does not go on forever. The secretions diminish and the pain returns after a while. This makes sense, as pain is one of the body's major signalling mechanisms when something is wrong. It would not make sense for our body to turn off the pain signal coming from a broken bone. So, the pain will return after the activity of the opiates is diminished.

12.3 Acupuncture

An interesting facet of this discussion on the body's opiates and the ability of the brain to modulate pain is that it begins to explain how acupuncture may work. Practised for centuries in China, acupuncture involves using fine needles that are stuck into patients at different points. With the needles in the body, pain is reduced to such an extent that surgery can be performed without anaesthesia. Many Western doctors and scientists scoffed at the notion of acupuncture working and ascribed it to one huge placebo effect. If they had investigated thoroughly, they would have discovered that veterinarians in China were using acupuncture to operate on animals. No cow, for example, will put up with the pain of surgery because of a placebo effect!

It turns out that acupuncture causes the release of large amounts of the endogenous opiates. This was proved by blocking the brain receptors for the opiates by a synthetic drug. The blocking cancels out the effect of any endogenous opiates. In such a case acupuncture no longer effectively blocks the pain. It is worth mentioning that the analgesic action of internal opiates is many times stronger than that of morphine; it is 200 times higher in the case of endorphins and more than 400 times higher in the case of dynorphins.

Left unanswered is the question—why does looking like a pincushion cause the release of the endogenous opiates? Answer from latest scientific research—don't know! To be more precise, several theories have been proposed to explain the action of acupuncture. They involve both the idea of activation of the opioids as well as suppression of pain signalling but no confirmed theory has been detailed in the literature.

Here is an interesting footnote to the story of stress and the release of endogenous opiates—fresh from winning the

Nobel Prize in 1972, it was Roger Guillemin* who demon-strated that stress triggers the release of beta-endorphin from the pituitary gland.

---

* Roger Guillemin was the scientist who discovered that the brain con-trols the various hormone secretions.

Chapter 13 Aging

This chapter covers a topic different from the rest of the book. Typically, we look at some important system in the body and examine the effects of stress or stress response. In this section, we are going to take a look at the big picture and deal with the whole body but from the point of view of examining the effects of stress on the aging process. Two obvious questions arise:

- Does stress or the body's stress response accelerate the aging process?
- How does an older individual deal with stress?

Intuitively, the answer to the first question seems to be that stress does accelerate the aging process. We can all imagine scenarios where the body is stressed repeatedly and tries valiantly to fight off these stressors and fatigues from the effort. Net result: accelerated aging and a body suffering from various diseases as a result of the stress or the stress response.

The second question also seems to have an intuitive answer: we all know from experience that older people seem to slow down physically and mentally. It seems simple to assume that the older person is not in a position to deal effectively with stress.

Gerontologists—those studying the aging process—find that most of us will age gracefully and with a fair degree of success. We may be so lucky as to be surrounded by our children and grandchildren whose health and vitality will give us a sense of immortality. Nevertheless, there are so many disastrous possibilities—wracking pain, dementia and a loss of control so severe that we cannot recognize our loved ones, muscles that do not respond to our will, ignored by our children and, worse, ill-treated by them, forced hospitalization and, worst of all, that aching sense that we are a burden to one and all. With such diverse possibilities, it is logical that many scientists are studying the aging process and how to avoid some of the worst outcomes.

One of the interesting things to note is that many studies of the aging process have to be carried out on laboratory animals with short life span or on primates in the wild. The difficulty in studying old people is that it is not often clear whether you are studying aging or the effects of some other disease that afflicts the person. Moreover, after a lifetime, many older people are on multiple medications (with their associated side-effects) and that increases the complexity of the studies. Laboratory animals with short life spans provide better models for study. Unfortunately, the study of aging in say, flies or mice, cannot reveal to us interesting results in terms of human aging (hard to study the psychological or emotional aspects of flies!). The best subjects are the primates (our close relatives from the evolutionary point of view). An old animal in the wild is supremely healthy—were it not, it would have been eaten a long time back. The studies on various aspects of the aging process in primates reveal a lot of interesting aspects and we will take a look at some of them in the subsequent sections.

From an evolutionary perspective, the problems with really aged organisms are relatively recent. Even today, the majority of the world population has a life span that does not leave many people in the very aged categories. The problems of aging appear in the affluent Western nations and the pockets of people who are categorized as upper income in other countries. A long life is still a luxury and not a basic fact of human life. No wonder that one of the most common forms of blessing is 'Live to be a centenarian'!

13.1 Managing Stress

One of the questions we posited at the start of this chapter was the ability of older individuals to deal with stress. The short answer is that they deal poorly with stress and the long answer is the rest of this section. The inability of older individuals to deal effectively with stress fits in with our intuition and observation of aged persons as vulnerable and fragile. To put it in perspective, almost all the systems of the body of older people work as they do for young people. But bring in a stressor[1] and the aged organism is likely to fail. Consider the scenario of an individual stressed by a sudden drop in temperature.

---

[1] It can be any type of stressor—physical, psychological or cognitive—and the effects are just the same. For example, time pressure, a novel situation or physical discomfort and the aged organism will not cope well.

Figure 13.1: Stress Response of Young and Aged Individuals

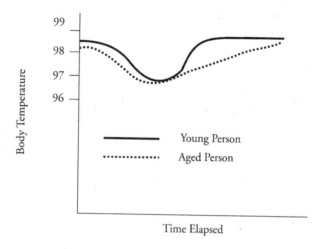

Figure 13.1 clearly shows that it takes longer for the older individual to regain normal temperature than a younger one. This takes us back to our definition of stress as anything that causes the body to be thrown out of allostasis; it seems older individuals take longer to regain allostasis than younger ones. In other studies, scientists measured the performance of different individuals in taking tests. The results are the same in the absence of stress. If the same tests are administered under stressful conditions (in noisy surroundings, under severe time pressure, etc.), the performance of old and young persons declines. The thing to note is that the performance drops to a greater extent in the older person. The reason for this poor performance seems to be the lack of sufficient

stress response. All the hormonal systems of the stress response have problems and the net result is that the older individuals cope poorly with stress. In some cases, there is enough hormonal secretion but the various cells are not responding to that signal.[2]

The stress response in the older individual usually continues even after the stressor has finished. It takes longer for the body to return to normal after the stressful period. This has been observed in many animal studies—stress young and old individuals and they may have roughly the same stress response. In the case of the older individual, it takes longer for the system to return to normal. It should be clear that secreting stress hormones in the absence of a stressor is a generally bad idea and can lead to many of the problems that we have discussed so far.

Older individuals have higher levels of stress-response hormones even in their normal resting state. The levels of epinephrine and norepinephrine are higher in older individuals in their resting states. Do older individuals pay the price for having their stress response turned on even during their rest time? The answer is yes. For example, the higher blood pressure seen in many older people can be linked to the higher levels of epinephrine and norepinephrine.

---

[2] This is the case with the cardiovascular system. With the onset of a stressor, epinephrine and norepinephrine are secreted to the same extent in both old and young persons. It is just that the heart and the blood vessels do not respond as vigorously to the hormonal signal in the older person.

13.2 Can Stress Accelerate Aging?

Intuitively, we all recognize that there is a connection between how we live and how we die. It then makes sense that if we are stressed during our youth, it will have an impact on how we age and how fast that takes place. At the beginning of the 20th century, Rubner, a German physiologist came up with the idea of living beings having a fixed time for which a body can go on. His main hypothesis was that an organism could carry on an activity for a specific number of times and, after that time; wear and tear would cause it to fail. For example, the heart can beat only so many times before it will fail. Using studies[3] he conducted about the heartbeats, breaths and various parameters in animals, he calculated lifetime number of heartbeats, metabolic rate and other parameters. For example, an elephant with 35 beats per minute lives a lot longer than say a rat with 400 beats a minute (the rat uses up its allocation of heartbeats faster). He theorized that this was the real explanation why some species live longer than others. It was obvious that similar thinking could be applied to individuals within the same species to explain the difference in life span. Subsequent studies and research have demonstrated the fallacies in Rubner's hypothesis and it is not considered credible anymore. Modern theory is that it is the long-term exposure to various stress-response hormones that can accelerate aging.

---

[3] It should come as no surprise that such studies are extremely difficult to undertake and that not many people have attempted to replicate them.

One particular case is interesting and worth examining separately. This has to do with the release of glucocorticoids during stress. The brain controls the release of the glucocorticoids by secreting corticotrophin releasing factor (CRF), which, in turn, signals the pituitary to release the glucocorticoids. How does the brain decide when there are enough glucocorticoids in the blood? Recall from Section 3.5 the mechanism for controlling hormone release. The brain controls the release of CRF (and, in turn, the glucocorticoids) using a negative feedback loop. The portion of the brain that senses the levels of glucocorticoids is the hypothalamus. It turns out that older people have a damaged hypothalamus. This will account for the higher levels of glucocorticoids even during normal times. It is like a leaky water tank and the feedback system is faulty. What could have caused the failure of the feedback system? The answer is not definite but the most likely culprit is the glucocorticoids during earlier chronic stress! This means that a lifetime of being exposed to glucocorticoids will lead to hippocampal damage which will lead to more glucocorticoids being released in the bloodstream—a frightening cascade!

13.3 Planning to Run a Marathon?

We all understand that we slow down as we age. As the body ages it seems to lose some of its capacity and it takes longer to get things done. I still remember my days from school when I would get up and be ready in 15 minutes. These days it takes me over an hour to do the same things and get ready for office. This point is also brought home when engaged in sports or during exercise. Setting out to beat a personal best established when our legs were years younger, we fall short and become convinced that we simply did not perform at our best.

Dr Ray C. Fair knows the agony, and he has a soothing explanation. Dr Fair is a professor of economics at Yale University, best known for devising a mostly accurate formula to predict winners of US presidential elections. He is also the finisher of 17 marathons and counting; and he has turned his social scientist's eye to a question that many serious runners have considered: how can you keep racing against yourself long after you can no longer catch yourself?

His answer comes in the form of a research paper he has written. Studying world records for runners all the way up to 92 years old, Dr Fair has developed tables that try to track the body's physical deterioration and set an ever-moving target.

If a 50-year-old finishes a marathon in 4 hours, 10 years after having run it in 3 hours 45 minutes, for instance, she can know that she is aging no more quickly than the world's fleetest runners.

Having been published in *The Review of Economics and Statistics*, Dr Fair's work has an academic credibility rare in matters of sport. But his tables are also part of a growing effort to help runners track their times over a lifetime.

Dr Fair became interested in the topic in the 1980s, when he realized that the national circuit of masters races, open to men older than 40 and women older than 35 and divided into age divisions, had created enough data for him to perform the calculations. He studied the tables published by the masters group and decided to approach the problem with the same rigorous technique, known as regression analysis that is at the heart of much economic research. He devised a set of tables that show the deterioration in performance as we age. The tables show the equivalent time (at different ages) for somebody at the peak running ages of the 20s and 30s. A five-hour finish, after all, is much more impressive for a 70-year-old than for a 30-year-old. These tables show a gradual decline in performance between the ages of 30 and 60. Sometime after that there is a big decline and then the rate of decline also increases in the next 10 to 15 years. This result is in line with our intuitive feeling for our decline in performance. Though these tables have been published for runners, the decline in performance (in percentage terms) should be applicable to other sports or physical activities.

It is interesting to note that underlying all the research, of course, is an assumption that ordinary people—or at least ordinary marathon runners—age at the same rate as elite athletes. If that is not the case, Dr Fair's tables and the masters tables would be setting the bar at the wrong place for most people. Scientists have yet to agree on an answer, however.

13.4 Bizarre Deaths

As an interesting aside and also due to the role of the principal stress-response hormone—glucocorticoids, we will take a brief look at some animals in which the males die soon after mating. Some species of salmon and some Australian marsupial mice have a bizarre life cycle where they die soon after mating. Researchers studying this phenomenon identified the glucocorticoids as the chief culprit and found excessive levels of the hormone in the males soon after mating. In other experiments, scientists found that cutting off the adrenals (stopping the release of glucocorticoids altogether) prevented the males from dying immediately after mating. Other than the mice or the salmon looking for the fountain of youth, there is no direct application to humans as we age gradually and not in some catastrophic events over a period of days. This is interesting information and I find it fascinating that in the history of evolution the same bizarre pattern of dying has evolved in two unrelated species.

This chapter has only briefly covered the two aspects of aging that are most likely affected by stress – the inadequate coping of the aged individual and the acceleration in aging due to the higher levels of stress hormones. This field is still open, as it is only in the last two decades or so that it has become quite common for people to live till 80 or 90 years. As advances in medicines and health care increase the average life span, many new aspects of the aging process will be apparent. One thing will not change—it is the way we live that will determine how we age and die. The old adage of 'you reap what you sow' will always hold true.

Chapter 14	Stress Management— A Scientific Background

The 1930s and the 1940s saw a great deal of scientific progress in the field of stress physiology after Selye demonstrated the effects of stress on rats. Scientists determined the main hormones released in response to stress were epinephrine, glucocorticoids and prolactin. Additional research uncovered the superb control mechanisms of the body that regulate the amount of these hormones released into the bloodstream. In engineering jargon there are *multiple feedback domains* for each hormone. In lay terms, it means that the brain uses a variety of techniques to regulate the quantity of hormones. Sometimes, it measures the actual quantity of the hormone in the blood; at other times, it may use the rate of change of the hormone in the blood, etc. The body not only can sense something stressful, but is also amazingly accurate at measuring just how far and how fast the stressor is throwing the body out of allostatic balance.

The early scientific literature on stress is dominated by research in the engineering aspects of the stress response and the various feedback systems that are present. Unfortunately, for the scientists, some everyday examples opened up another set of factors that control stress response. Take an example of a small child getting an injection. The stress response can be fairly easily calculated and a neat mathematical model can explain it. Now if the same child has a loving parent who will comfort it, the obvious result is that the child will show less of a stress response. The critical fact here is that body's stress response (physiological response) can be controlled (modulated) by psychological factors. In other words, the stress response can be made bigger or smaller depending on purely psychological factors. Inevitably, the next step in this process was demonstrated—in the absence of any change in the physiological reality (i.e., no disruption in the allostasis of the body), purely psychological factors could trigger a stress response.

One of the early scientists to have discovered this phenomenon was Yale physiologist John Mason. He even proclaimed that all stress response was psychological. Obviously, there was a great deal of scientific debate about the nature of the stress response with Selye leading the group that said it was not purely psychological. In defence, they cited studies that showed that a stress response is generated among patients administered anesthesia during surgery immediately after the first incision is made. The current consensus is that some psychological factors can modulate the stress response.

The above paragraph discussed a very powerful concept from the point of view of the person suffering from stress. If we can identify the psychological factors that affect stress response, we can put those in practice and avoid the trouble caused by it. At first glance, it might seem that determining the psychological factors involved in stress response might be a mushy, *touchy-feely* field of psychologists and therapists. But that is not the case and a solid body of elegant scientific experiments were used to identify the psychological factors. We will take a look at some of those experiments and see how they can help us in formulating coping strategies.

In one of the experiments, a rat received a mild electric shock (comparable to a human being receiving a static shock from a silk material or woollen carpet during winter). Over a series of these shocks the rat develops a prolonged stress response—its heart rate and glucocorticoids secretion go up, the probability of getting ulcer soars and a number of other diseases afflict the rat.

A second rat gets the same set of shocks—same intensity, duration and frequency. Its body is thrown out of allostasis to the same extent as the first rat. The only difference is that the second rat has a small piece of wood to chew on. Every time, it gets a shock, it can run to the wood and gnaw on it. The rat shows a low stress response. In the actual experiment, the scientists were examining the probability of getting ulcers. For the rat with a piece of wood to gnaw on, the probability of getting ulcers was dramatically lower than the one with no wood. The second rat had an *outlet for frustration*. Other types of outlets work as well—let the stressed rat eat something, drink something or sprint on a running wheel and the likelihood of developing ulcers drops. We humans deal better with stressors when we have an outlet for our frustration. We are smart enough to imagine some of those outlets and get some relief. We are all familiar with the anecdotes of prisoners of war who spend hours imagining their favourite hobby to alleviate the prolonged and stressful period of captivity.

Another facet of this outlet for frustration was uncovered in experiments where the stressed rat could bite a smaller rat. To put it in scientific jargon, the rat shows stress-induced displacement aggression. The fact is that it works amazingly well in reducing the stress response of the rat receiving the shock. In fact, such displacement aggression is a real primate speciality. Baboons, monkeys and a host of other animals demonstrate the same stress-induced aggression towards weaker, lower ranked animals. Depressingly, we humans are good at it too. Fortunately for the human race, a better strategy than beating up smaller persons is that of *social networking*. It helps to have a shoulder to cry on, a hand to hold, a loved one to listen to you, someone to hug you and tell you that it will be all right. In another series of subtle studies, volunteers were exposed to various stressors—giving a public speech, or perform mental arithmetic in a noisy and crowded area, arguing with strangers—with or without a supportive friend present. In all cases, social support translated into less of a cardiovascular stress response. Persistent differences in degrees of social support can influence human physiology as well. For example, within the same family, step-children exhibit higher levels of stress hormones than among the biological children.

The studies on rats were performed with another set of controls. The rat gets the same shocks as before. However, before each shock, it hears a warning bell. Not surprisingly, the rate of ulcers drops. There is now *predictability* as to when the rat is administered an electric shock. It is not so much that the predictability helps reduce the effects of the shock but it allows the rat to rest and relax between the shocks. As another variant on the helpfulness of predictability, organisms will eventually get used to a stressor if it is applied over and over. The typical example given is that of army recruits as they learn to jump from a plane with a parachute. At the start of the training, the anticipatory stress response is very high. By the end of the training, the response is almost nonexistent. We will see in a later section, the use of this technique to reduce anxiety and fear. Another experiment reveals an interesting facet of predictability. A rat is given small amounts of food at regular intervals. The rat eats it happily and in scientific terms it is called *intermittent reinforcement schedule*. Next, the pattern of delivery is changed from regular to random. The same amount of food is delivered over the course of time but the interval between deliveries is random. The rat experiences a stress response. There is not a single stressful thing going on in the rat's life. In the absence of any stressor, loss of predictability triggers a stress response.

There are even circumstances in which people subjected to a lower state of a stressor can experience higher incidence of stress-related disease due to unpredictability. It would be easy to design an experiment with rats to prove this point. Unfortunately, a human version of this scenario took place during the World War II. In that instance, the Nazis bombed London with clockwork regularity every night. The suburbs of London received a lot less bombing but it was very irregular (a high degree of unpredictability). It turns out that the ulcer rates were far higher in the suburbs than in London. An interesting postscript to this story—the ulcer rates dropped to pre-war levels after a few months of bombing! We have heard of stories of prisoners awaiting execution who demand an end to their appeals to higher courts to avoid the uncertainty. It seems like the waiting and unpredictability is worse than death!

Continuing with our rat studies, another related facet of psychology could be demonstrated. Give a rat a series of shocks as before. This time, use a rat that has been trained to press a lever to avoid the shock. Take away the lever, shock it, and the rat develops a massive stress response and major ulcers develop. Give the rat a lever to press even though it has been disconnected from the shock mechanism and it still helps. Down goes the stress response. Thus, the exercise of control is not critical; rather it is the belief that you have the control.

Some researchers have pointed out that loss of predictability and loss of control share a common element—novelty. Others have emphasized that these types of stressors cause arousal and vigilance, as you search for the new rules of predictability and control. I think both these views are just different aspects of the same set of issues.

As we saw above, there are some powerful psychological factors that can trigger a stress response on their own, or make another stressor seem more stressful—loss of control or predictability, loss of outlet for frustration or source of support, or a perception that things are getting worse. These factors help in partly explaining how we all go through life full of stressors, yet differ so dramatically in our response to them. In engineering terms, it is as if we differ in the psychological filters through which we perceive the stressors in our world.

The experiments discussed above provide the foundation for formulating strategies to cope with stress. The strategies will involve some or all of these psychological variables, depending on the person and the stressor but they will help in reducing the ill-effects of the stress response.

Chapter 15 | Techniques for Stress Management

The central theory of this book is the irony of the stress response—it evolved in physical environments very different from the social and psychological ones of today. Instead of being stalked by a saber-toothed tiger, today it is traffic jams, board exams, terrorist threats, bomb attacks in the city and worries over money.

With stress, your heart pounds, chest heaves and muscles tighten. Senses sharpen; time slips into slow motion, and you become impervious to pain. Under conditions of physical stress, this would be an appropriate healthy reaction because now you are prepared to do battle. The trouble is, however, that you are probably still sitting in your car or at your desk—stewing in your own juices. It's time to relieve your stress.

Bear in mind that an appropriate stress response is a healthy and necessary part of life. As we have discussed repeatedly, one of the things it does is to release norepinephrine—the principal excitatory neurotransmitter. Norepinephrine is needed to create new memories. It improves mood. Problems feel more like challenges, which encourages creative thinking that stimulates your brain to grow new connections within it. Stress management is the key, not stress elimination. The challenge in this day and age is to not let the sympathetic nervous system stay chronically aroused. This may require knowledge of techniques that work to activate your relaxation response. Here you will find a variety of techniques and fascinating studies to help you manage stress in your daily life.

15.1 Physical Exercise

One of the most obvious ways to relieve stress is to do what the body was meant to do under those circumstances—physical activity. More precisely, exercise proves to be an excellent mechanism for stress reduction.

Four related studies done in 1999 at the University of Colorado at Boulder looked at how regular exercise changes physiological responses to stress from the brain, hormonal system, and immune system. 'Our goal is to understand how regular, moderate, physical activity alters the stress response by examining the entire system, from the brain to the individual cells,' says Assistant Professor Monika Fleshner. Doctors know that people who exercise regularly are less likely to fall sick after stressful situations. On the other hand, exposure to mental or physical stress increases a person's susceptibility to illness or disease, she said. The four studies and many others have shown that exercise helps:

- to lower the level of norepinephrine released in response to stress;

- to improve infection fighting capability;
- to significantly reduce the negative effects of stress, including the suppression of cell division, decreases cytokines, and increases production of stress proteins.

Exercise Combats Depression Studies

Exercise not only defuses a stressful situation, it prepares you to better cope with future stress and helps fight depression. The World Health Organization warns that by the year 2020, depression will be the second leading cause of death and disability in the world—primarily due to more stressful lifestyles, poverty, and violence.

When University of California at San Diego researchers kept track of more than 900 older adults whose average age was 70, they found that those who exercised regularly had the best moods a decade later. In contrast, men and women who never exercised, or quit during the study, were more likely to develop a depressive mood. One of the study's authors, Dr Donna Kritz-Silverstein, stated that this 'shows there's a beneficial effect, but to reap the benefits you have to keep exercising'—especially with regular activities that break a sweat, such as brisk walking. An important point the author has emphasized is that 'starting exercise at an older age can be just as beneficial'.

A Finnish study had similar results. When depressive symptoms were compared with exercise intensity in 663 elderly people over an eight-year-period, active physical exercise was associated with better mental health. Paivi Lampinen and colleagues at the University of Jyvaskyla concluded that 'age-related decrease in the intensity of physical exercise increases the risk of depressive symptoms among older adults'.

Practical tips for using exercise to reduce stress

- Do exercises that work your leg muscles.
- Jog in place—do spot running.
- Climb stairs or use a stair-stepper.
- Take a brisk walk.
- Use a treadmill—it works for lab rats.
- Use short bursts of muscular energy like the PT exercises we learned in school.

15.2 Massage

Massage reduced levels of glucocorticoids and epinephrine in depressed mothers with infants. A study at the Touch Research Institute at the University of Miami Medical School found that massage therapy also improved sleep and reduced the mothers' depression.

Pre-schoolers who received a 15-minute massage scored better on tests of cognitive performance compared to children who just read stories with an adult for the 15 minutes prior to testing.

Recall from our discussion on pain and how massage helps temporarily relieve the throbbing pain. Besides reducing the pain, it helps us to relax and better focus on our activities afterwards.

15.3 Breathe to Relax

Nature has provided a perfect way to help activate our relaxation response, and it involves an involuntary bodily function that we can also consciously control—our breathing. Nothing is more convenient than using our breath to bring ourselves back into balance. Whether quieting a rapid fearful breath or boosting a shallow anxious one, just a few mindful breaths can shift our experience.

Breath Control Power Studies

After individuals with normal blood pressure were subjected to mental stress for 5 minutes, it took an average of 3.7 minutes for their blood pressure to return to normal. But when they practised deep breathing, it returned to normal in 2.7 minutes, an almost 25 per cent reduction in time.

Rapid Relaxation Breath

The Stress Management and Counseling Center in New York recommends a breathing technique for rapid relaxation. According to programme director and practising psychologist Allen Elkin, Ph.D.: 'You take a deep breath, deeper than normal, and hold it in until you notice a little discomfort. At the same time, squeeze your thumb and first finger together (as if you were making the okay sign) for six or seven seconds. Then exhale slowly through your mouth, release the pressure in your fingers, and imagine all your tension to drain out. Repeat these deep breaths three times to extend the relaxation. With each breath, allow your shoulders to droop, your jaw to drop and your body to relax.'

A Breathing Exercise You Can Do Right Now—

The first step is to bring your breathing under control:

- Exhale completely.
- Then slowly breathe in through your nose.
- Expand your diaphragm/belly to bring air into the lower portion of your lungs.
- As you gradually fill your lungs from bottom to top, expand your chest.
- At the end, lift your shoulders for a last bit of volume.
- Briefly pause your breathing.
- Then relax and let the air flow smoothly and fully out through your mouth.
- Pull in your stomach at the end to expel the last bit of air.
- Enjoy the emptiness for a few seconds.
- Then begin another breath.
- As you do this a few times, pay attention to the sound and sensation of your breath. If you get light-headed at first, then breathe normally.

15.4 Psychological Techniques

Reading through the literature on stress, we can find some psychological answers to coping with stress that are far from simple to implement in everyday life. They emphasize the importance of manipulating feelings of control, predictability, outlets for frustration, social connectedness, and the perception of whether things are worsening or improving. These messages are used in stress management seminars, therapy sessions and many books on the topic. In one form or the other, these same thoughts are propounded by motivitational speakers and new-age gurus where they emphasize finding means to gain at least some degree of control in difficult situations, viewing bad situations as discrete events rather than permanent or pervasive, finding appropriate outlets for frustration and means of social support and solace in difficult times. Many speakers use glib phrases and nice-sounding simple sentences to capture the basic techniques. Personally, I am very sceptical about such glib talk. It is nice to enunciate a general principle but that leaves many ordinary people clueless as to how it should be implemented in practice. Here is my personal list of mental strategies gleaned from the literature. I have tried to avoid making generalizations or offering vague prescriptions. The first step is to accurately recognize the signs of stress and to identify the situations most responsible for it. There are some ways to proceed after that:

- *One successful strategy is to find an outlet for life's frustrations.* Typically, many people find a hobby a nice diversion. Try and choose an activity that will require some active participation. For example, watching TV is not a good choice. Drawing, craft, music (playing not just listening), hiking, knitting, crochet, playing any sports are all excellent choices. Many people may find regular prayer and worship (performing 'pooja') or visiting the temple as an excellent alternative. Set aside a time to do it and do it regularly. A simple word of caution: make the outlet a benign one for those around you and do not stress your family while doing it. Practising to play the bugle may be good for you but doing it in a small apartment in the city is not a good idea. Choose an outlet that you find personally pleasing. Prayer, meditation, reading, classical music, and sports—each may help some people but not others. In subsequent sections, we will give some information on these techniques and some of the scientific studies conducted to study their effects. If someone tries to sell you some activity as being helpful for stress reduction, you should read the fine print carefully and not buy the over-hyped claims. There is no scientific study showing the benefit of one form over the other in reducing the effects of stress. There is only anecdotal evidence and it should be treated with healthy scepticism. It is best to trust one's own instincts and go with what seems best.

- Many times in life we are faced with situations that seem hopeless. Accidental death, disability, terminal illnesses are situations that are beyond our control. In the face of terrible news that is beyond control, beyond prevention, beyond healing, a state of denial may be the only answer. Such denial is not only permissible but may be the only means of maintaining sanity. This point was brought home in the case of a colleague whose teenage daughter died in an accident. The parents were too distraught and there were no words of consolation that could be offered. For a few months, they basically were in denial about their daughter's death and it allowed them to function. Later, they slowly came to grips with the situation. But in the initial phases, the denial was their only way to maintain sanity.

- In the face of problems that are not life-and-death situations, one should hope, but protectively and rationally. *Find ways to view even the most stressful of situations as holding promise of improvement but do not deny the possibility that things will not improve.* Balance these two opposing trends carefully. Hope for the best and let that dominate most of your emotions. At the same time, let one small piece of you prepare for the worst. This was clearly illustrated in the case of a friend whose four-year-old son was diagnosed with leukaemia. It was diagnosed early and the prognosis was good. However, there was always the possibility that it may not be cured. In such situations it is best to have cautious optimism.

- Those who cope with stress successfully tend to seek control over future events in the face of stressors. They do not try to control, in the present, things that have already come to pass. They do not try to control future events that are uncontrollable and do not try to fix things that are not broken or that are broken beyond repair. When faced with a large wall of stressors, one should not assume that there will be a breakthrough, one single controlling solution that will make the wall disappear. It is futile to wait for the *avatar* or 'redeemer' to set everything right in one moment. For many people, we see that they wait for a miracle or some sudden change in fortune as the solution to all their problems. This hope sustains them in their daily life but does not improve their lot.

Success will be built one brick at a time. Assume that the stress wall can be scaled by a series of footholds of control, each one small but still capable of giving support.

- *It is important to find sources of social affiliation.* In my opinion, this is one of the most successful strategies for coping with stress. Evolution has favoured humans with all the tools for socialization and it will be the best tool for coping with stress. Even in this age of increasingly individualistic view of most people, we yearn to be a part of something larger than ourselves. The key is not to mistake true affiliation for mere socializing. It is necessary to be patient; most of us will probably spend a lifetime learning how to be truly good friends and spouses.

Friends who make you laugh are one of life's greatest blessings. Here's where the right social network pays off. *One of the most important anti-stress coping skills is to develop a social support system, including pets.* When 1,200 septuagenarians (people in their 70s) were studied over seven years, emotional support was significantly correlated with better cognitive function, such as language, verbal and non-verbal memory, abstract reasoning, and spatial ability.

Researchers at the University of Zurich observed that a friend's supportive presence might work with hormones in the body to reduce stress. Men were less stressed when their best friend was present or when they were given a nasal of dose of oxytocin, an anti-stress hormone. Just the presence of a best friend, however, was better than oxytocin alone at reducing stress.

In very simple terms, in the face of adversity, we need to show flexibility, resiliency and pick our battles carefully. A Quaker prayer puts these same sentiments in a far more beautiful and elegant manner—

In the face of strong winds, let me be a blade of grass.
In the face of strong walls, let me be a gale of wind.

Some other practical suggestions include:

Derail Your Train of Thoughts

Try to slowdown and stop the everyday onslaught of thought that wears you out—especially the kind of circular thinking that gets you nowhere. Recall our discussion on 'over-thinking' from chapter 10 on depression, especially for women. It is important to avoid getting into such state of circular thinking that does not lead to any obvious solution. Perhaps there's a simple thought or quote you can use to help you derail your train of thoughts and initiate your relaxation response.

The Practice of Meditation

Unlike prayer, where you do the talking, meditation is more akin to listening. Your breath is the most natural thing to tune in to. Just observe your breathing. Listen to the sound it makes and feel the sensation it creates. This leads you into a meditative state. If thoughts enter your mind, just let them go. Passively disregard them. Instead, stay with your breath. Let it settle into its own circular rhythm.

One or two daily sessions of meditation—preferably at the same time every day—will change the way your body responds to stress because the effects of one session can last throughout the day. Having written the last paragraph, I have to confess that 'letting go' of your thoughts is far easier to write in a book than in actual practice. Many a times, I have experimented and tried a variety of techniques to let go of my thoughts during meditation. No luck—I am still stuck with all my thoughts. With my limited experience and poor understanding of the meditation techniques, I have kept this discussion to a minimum. There are obviously many nuances to meditation, and a qualified teacher may be advisable. There are very few rigorous scientific studies on the benefits of meditation. Alternatively, you can follow some of the other techniques discussed in this chapter and get the stress-reducing benefits. My personal favourite—regular physical exercise. One of the best techniques for combining the advantages of meditation with the physical benefits of exercise is the practice of 'yoga'. There is no question about the advantages of regular yoga on improving both physical and mental health. There are many excellent books available on the subject. It is one of the best techniques for those who can take it up and the benefits will be immediate and long lasting.

Brain Mapped During Meditation Studies

In a study at the Medical College of Georgia, scientists discovered that the daily practice of transcendental meditation kept blood vessels open, thus significantly lowering the blood pressure of meditators compared with those who just relaxed as completely as possible.

Harvard Medical School researchers used functional Magnetic Resonance Imaging (MRI) to identify and characterize the brain regions that are active during a simple form of meditation. Significant signal increases were observed in the pre-frontal cortex, hippocampus, and the cortex. According to the researchers, this indicates that 'meditation activates neural structures involved in attention and control of the autonomic nervous system.' A caveat that we discussed earlier is in order. These are only a few studies that show the effects of meditation. Just because some portions of the brain are activated does not mean that a specific action like control of the autonomic system is happening. We should accept these claims with a healthy dose of scepticism. Only if it works in our own case, should we continue with the meditation.

Some practical tips for stress reduction using our thoughts and emotions:

- See problems as opportunities or at least break a problem into manageable chunks.
- Do not take all things personally.
- There is no right answer to every problem.
- It is not a perfect world.
- Let go of some things.
- This too shall pass.
- Refute negative thoughts.
- Stop over generalizing.
- Control yourself, not others.
- Be yourself.

15.5 Relieve Your Stress Through Senses

Our senses are constantly bombarded with noises and smells. Some are pleasant and some are invasive. While much of this sensory input may be beyond our control, we can use the senses to relieve our stress, including our sense of humour!

Getting a little poetical here, find the muse whose music best conducts your endocrine ensemble of stress-relieving hormones. Whatever kind of music soothes your savage beast—Indian classical, Hindi filmi, Jazz, R&B—let it shift your brain into its parasympathetic symphony. Toning, chanting, and other self-generated sounds have transforming effects on the mind and emotions. 'The most powerful aspect of music is rhythm,' says music therapy Professor Ron Borczon. 'Rhythm will help you get more excited when sped up; when slowed down, it helps the body calm down.'

Use Your Sense of Humour

Before you react to some stressor, first try becoming an observer whose job it is to find the humour in the situation. Seek belly laughs which make you feel good, as well as more stress proof. The pioneering work of Norman Cousins demonstrated the value of laughter in stress reduction. The next time you feel road-rage or some other stressor starting to rear its ugly tail, just start making a funny noise. Such sounds are incompatible with anger.

Crying Relieves Stress Chemistry

Crying is another one of nature's stress-relieving strategies. Psychiatric chemist, William Frey, Ph.D., showed that not all tears are the same. Unlike tears caused by eye irritants, emotional tears contain abundant amounts of epinephrine and other stress-related chemicals. This should not be taken to mean that we start crying every time we get stressed. On the other hand, many people think of crying as a sign of weakness and will do anything to avoid being seen with tears in their eyes. Neither extreme is correct and we should view crying as healthy response to a particularly bad situation that will help relieve the stress temporarily.

15.6 Reminder

The previous sections covered a number of techniques and methods for dealing with psychological stress. In each instance where a technique has been suggested, there is a reference to some scientific study or research to back up that finding. A caveat is on order here—typically, there are only one or two studies to back up the claim. Further, many of the studies are conducted by organizations that are advocating a particular technique or methodology for stress relief. Typically, these are commercial organizations and they have an interest in selling some product or service. It is best to adopt a very sceptical attitude towards such research. Never buy or blindly accept some claim as being scientifically proven when made as part of some sales pitch. I am repeating this point—there are no magic cures and no instant solutions.

Chronic psychological stress causes the problems and the solutions are not going to work instantaneously.

Stress management will require persistence, positive attitude and a willingness to change things for the better. It is this ability to view the world events through positive psychological filters that will mark the true success in stress management.

15.7 Unconventional Technique

The preceding sections have given a number of suggestions to reduce stress. In this section, we will cover a technique that is quite controversial but claimed to be effective. This technique, advocated by the psychologist David H. Barlow for treating anxiety disorders, is surprisingly simple to explain, although its philosophical and clinical implications are anything but. He aims to reduce anxiety not by teaching any of the customary relaxation techniques discussed previously involving calming mantras or soothing imagery, but by doing just the opposite: forcing the patient to repeatedly face his most dreaded situation, so that, eventually, he becomes accustomed to the sensation of terror. This treatment promises to be psychotherapy's ultimate fast track. While many clinicians praise its well-documented results, others take a dimmer view of what one clinician characterizes 'torture, plain and simple.'

To give an idea of Barlow's technique, we will look at an example of one of his patients. The patient is a 30-year-old woman who is afraid of flying. Barlow's technique calls for her to take repeated plane trips till she overcomes her fear. In this particular case the patient was cured after eight trips or so. This technique can be compared to vaccinations for infectious diseases. In vaccination, we take a dead or weakened virus so that the body can learn how to fight the real thing. Barlow's technique claims to vaccinate the mind. There is considerable clinical research to show the efficacy of this treatment method. The supporters of this method claim that modifications of this technique can be applied to other psychological diseases like depression. However, this is not very convincing. After all, depression is precisely a problem of meaninglessness, whereas anxiety, one might say, is a problem of excess meaning. What good would it do to teach a melancholic patient that her thoughts are null and void? She already believes that acutely. Furthermore, those in a state of severe sadness would probably lack the high, hopeful motivation that characterizes Barlow's anxiety patients. You can get a jittery, willful person to fly repeatedly to overcome the fear of flying, but could a depressed person really find the energy to care?

I will conclude by saying that for some stressors (fearful situations), Barlow's technique may help some people in overcoming their fear. If it does not work for us, we should not feel that we are weak or do not have the mental strength to just overcome our fear—that reasoning would be totally incorrect.

In conclusion it is important to note a few things. Stress is everywhere. Every twinge of dysfunction in our bodies is not a manifestation of stress-related disease. It is true that the world is full of bad things that we can cope with by altering our outlook and psychological makeup but it is also full of awful things that cannot be eliminated by a change in attitude no matter how heroically, fervently or ritualistically we may wish. Here is the important point, once we are actually sick with the illness, none of the stress management techniques can provide immediate relief. Once diabetes has set in or the depressive attacks occur, treatment with medicines is our only option. Stress management should be used as a preventive treatment. We have the capacity to lead our lives and make such changes that we prevent some of the stress-related problems before they turn into full-fledged diseases.

Chapter 16 | The 'P' Word

Healthy poverty but lame riches

This widely-used proverb in Marathi is cited often to show how futile it is to pursue riches. The implication is clear: Poor people with a clear conscience are healthier and lead better lives than the rich folk who spend their time amassing their fortune and suffer from poor health. Nothing could be further from the truth!

In this chapter, we will take a look at one social stressor that has an impact on a person's life. Until now, we have looked at stressors (stress responses) that affect particular systems for some periods of time. Unfortunately, for a majority of the population in our country, there is one stressor that cannot be eliminated or minimized and none of the stress management techniques discussed are relevant. Yes, I am talking of poverty. Page after page of this book has discussed the impact of chronic stress on different systems in the body and the horrendous things that can happen because of it. Left unsaid was the tacit assumption that these stressors, though chronic, would eventually stop. The stress management techniques that emphasized outlets of frustration, predictability and sense of control were really applicable to a world where the individual does not face a daily struggle just to survive. A starving person in Orissa or a bonded labourer in a poor state like Bihar has no use for these stress management techniques. Their lives are filled with unpredictable events over which they have no control; they can barely make ends meet and starvation is not uncommon. Their conditions exacerbate the effects of any additional stressors they may face—prolonged illnesses in the family, drought, flooding, or any number of factors beyond their control; mind numbing hours spent working in a field or a squalid hut doing some manual work under difficult conditions; a life spent taking orders from others, jobs lost at the first hint of trouble and always wondering if the money will last till the end of the month or even till the end of the week. When almost your entire waking hours are spent in earning a living, it is impossible to have a hobby or some other outlet for your frustration. There is a major lack of social support—your entire family is working or trying to find some work. There is no time left to unwind, sit together with your loved ones and discuss problems. Free time, if any, is likely to be spent in fighting and drunken squabbles!

I have included this as the last chapter as none of the techniques in this book can help the poor. We have developed a system of ignoring poverty in our midst. Most of us tend not to even notice the beggars surrounding our vehicles at the traffic lights. I hope this chapter will help in bringing home the dire effects of poverty and that the readers will show compassion and lend a helping hand to the millions of sufferers in this country.

16.1 Stress and Poverty

Grinding poverty leads to a massive build-up of stress: but it is always difficult to carry out a study that will establish a direct correlation. One reason for this is that poverty comes with its hand-maiden—infectious diseases. There is one way out—for example, although considered one of the richest and technologically advanced countries, America has a dark underside. There are a number of poor people whose condition is very similar to that of the poor in many other countries. The Americans can spend considerable resources and study the problems of associated poverty. As one of my reviewers for this book suggested in jest—the only reason to include this section in the book is that data is readily available for poverty in America. That may be partly true but the real reason is that it helps to study the poverty in a rich country because all other factors have generally been eliminated. Let me explain. Say, you study the poor in Bihar and consider their average life span. Most of them still die from infectious diseases due to inhuman living conditions. So, you are studying the effects of a disease rather than poverty. In America, most of the infectious diseases have been eradicated; there is a minimum emergency health care available to all, hunger is non-existent and the contrast with the rest of the population is easily visible. The results can thus be directly ascribed to poverty and we can draw some useful lessons from that.

The important point to note is that those who are considered 'poor' in America do not face the sort of deprivation as the poverty stricken in India. In fact, the poor in America have more material things and access to support systems than most people in this country. Yet, the effects of poverty are damaging. One can only imagine how bad the situation must be for the nameless, faceless, poor huddled masses in this country.

Something is killing America's urban poor, but this is no ordinary epidemic. When diseases like AIDS, measles and polio strike, everyone's symptoms look more or less the same, but not in this case. It seems as if the aging process in some people has accelerated. Even teenagers are afflicted with numerous health problems including asthma, diabetes and high blood pressure. Poor urban blacks have the worst health of any ethnic group in America with the possible exception of native Americans. It makes you wonder whether there is something deadly in the American experience of urban poverty itself.

The neighbourhoods where the majority of the poor live, look the same all across the country, with bricked-up abandoned buildings, vacant storefronts, broken sidewalks and empty lots with mangy grass overgrowing the ruins of old cars, machine parts and heaps of garbage. Young men in black nylon skullcaps lurk around the pay phones on street corners waiting to complete drug deals. These neighbourhoods are as segregated from the more affluent, white sections of metropolitan New York as any township in South Africa under apartheid. Living in such neighbourhoods is assumed to predispose the poor to a number of social ills, including drug abuse, truancy and the persistent joblessness that draws young people into a long cycle of crime and incarceration. Now it turns out these neighbourhoods could be destroying people's health as well.

There are many different types of disadvantaged neighbourhoods in America, but poor urban minority localities seem to be especially unhealthy. Some of these neighbour-hoods have the highest mortality rates in the US, but this is not, as many believe, mainly because of drug overdoses and gunshot wounds. It is because of chronic diseases—mainly diseases of adulthood that are probably not caused by virus-es, bacteria or other infections and that include stroke, dia-betes, kidney disease, high blood pressure and certain types of cancer.

The problems start at birth. The black infant death rate in Westchester County (about 50 miles north of New York City) is almost three times as high as the rate for the county as a whole. Black youths in Harlem, central Detroit, the south side of Chicago and Watts have the same probability of dy-ing by age 45 as whites nationwide do by age 65, and most of this premature death is not due to violence, but illness. A third of poor black 16-year-old girls in urban areas will not reach their 65th birthdays. Four times as many people die of diabetes in the largely black area of central Brooklyn as on the predominantly white Upper East Side of Manhattan, and one in three adults in Harlem report having high blood pres-sure. In 1990, two New York doctors found that so many poor African-Americans in Harlem were dying young from heart disease, cancer and cirrhosis of the liver, that men there were less likely to reach the age of 65 than men in Bangladesh.

Since the days of slavery, physicians have noted that the health of impoverished blacks is, in general, worse than that of whites. Racist doctors proposed that the reasons were genetic, and that blacks were intrinsically inferior and physi-cally weaker than whites. But there is very little evidence that poor blacks or Hispanics are genetically predisposed to the vast majority of the afflictions from which they disproportionately suffer. As the living conditions of blacks have improved over the past century, their health improved in step; when conditions deteriorated, health deteriorated too. This has helped support the contention among researchers that chronic disease among minority groups is caused not by genes, but by something else.

In some ways, public health institutions in America are in the same position they were in 150 years ago. In the mid-19th century, public health boards were established to fight the great killers of the day—cholera and tuberculosis. The poor were more susceptible to these diseases then, just as they are more prone to chronic diseases now. And then, as now, the reasons were unknown. Some believed diseases were acts of God and the poor got what they deserved. If they would only drink less, go to church and stay out of brothels, they wouldn't get sick. Others maintained that the afflictions of poverty were environmental. A stinking mass of invisible vapour, referred to as 'miasma', hung in the air over the slums, they claimed, and sickened those who inhaled it.

It was not until the early 1880s, when the German scientist Robert Koch looked down his microscope at swirling cholera and tuberculosis bacteria, that everyone finally agreed about what was going on. The water the poor drank was full of sewage and contained deadly cholera germs; in overcrowded tenements, the poor breathed clouds of tuberculosis bacteria. Malnourished alcoholics tended to be more susceptible to these diseases, but immoral behaviour was not their primary cause. Nor was miasma. The primary cause was germs.

There is no germ theory for chronic diseases like stroke, heart disease, diabetes and cancer. We know something about what can aggravate these diseases—diet, smoking and so on—but not enough about why they are so much more common among people who live in certain neighbourhoods, or what makes, for example, a poor person who smokes the same number of cigarettes a day as a rich person more likely to get lung cancer. Or, why several research studies show that smoking, eating, drinking and exercise habits do not fully account for why rich people are healthier than poor people. Even the lack of health care cannot entirely explain the afflictions of the poor. Many poor people lack health insurance, and those who have it are often at the mercy of overworked doctors and nurses who provide indifferent care. However, inadequate health care cannot explain why so many of them get so sick in the first place.

Clearly, we need to examine this miasma with a different kind of microscope. The best we have at the moment are theories that fall into two main schools of thought. One school holds the view that the problem has mainly to do with stress; the other holds actual deprivation responsible. These two factors are often intertwined, but the emphasis is important. The poor have enormous family obligations. While the middle-class people are able to purchase childcare and care for elderly relatives, the poor cannot. The experience of racism and discrimination in everyday life is also still very real, and very stressful. Blacks are faced with a society that institutionalizes the idea 'that you are a menace—and that demeans you'. Nancy Krieger, a Harvard researcher, found that working-class

African-Americans who said they accepted unfair treatment as a fact of life had higher blood pressure than those who challenged it.

Some social scientists call the grinding everyday stress of being poor and marginalized in America 'weathering', a condition not unlike the effect of exposure to wind and rain on houses. Stress is subjective, a feeling, and it means different things to different people. Many researchers involved in public health research note that stress is like the miasma that was once thought to cause cholera in 19th-century slums. 'You can't see it, you can't really measure it, but it floats over certain people, especially the poor, and makes them sick.'

If 'weathering' and stress have their modern-day Robert Koch, he is probably Bruce McEwen, a neuroendocrinologist at Rockefeller University in New York. McEwen argues that stress hormones threaten the health of poor people, especially blacks and the Hispanic poor. As we have seen throughout this book, constant exposure to stress hormones impairs the immune system and damages the brain and other organs. Chronic stress also signals the body to accumulate abdominal fat around the waistline, which is more dangerous than fat that lies under the skin, or subcutaneous fat. Abdominal fat worsens many chronic health problems, including diabetes and heart disease, whereas subcutaneous fat does not.

Not everyone believes that stress is a major contributor to the health crisis among the poor. George Davey Smith, a professor of clinical epidemiology at the University of Bristol in England, believes that the poor live very stressful lives, and that racism is an everyday reality for many people. However, in his view—the second school of thought on the matter—the health crisis among the poor has more to do with living in a deprived environment.

A recent survey conducted in four regions of the US found that there were three times as many bars in poor neighbourhoods as in rich ones, and four times as many supermarkets in white neighbourhoods as in black ones. There are fewer parks in poor neighbourhoods as well, so it is more difficult to find open spaces in which to exercise, and many of them are dangerous. It was observed that 41 per cent of New York's public elementary schools have no consistent physical education programme. Public health campaigns that tell people to 'just say no' to smoking, or to change their diets and start exercising, can be cruel if they are indifferent to neighbourhood circumstances.

Many of the poor black people who are sick today grew up in the 1940s, 1950s and 1960s when many black people lived in overcrowded dwellings and were more prone than affluent whites to childhood infections. Some of these infections may have long-term effects on health. Adults, who were poor as children, even if they are not poor now, are also more prone to stroke, kidney disease and hypertensive heart disease. It is especially relevant at this point to discuss a very important study carried out on nuns as regards the effects of poverty. In this study of a group of Catholic sisters who had taken their vows in youth, the scientists found that their patterns of disease, aging, dementia and longevity itself were determined by their socio-economic status before they became nuns. This is an incredible finding—as the sisters after taking their vows had the same food, shared their living quarters and led the same life. The indelible mark of poverty from their ordinary lives could not be erased and the sisters from poor families had more diseases and other problems than their compatriots who came from average households. It seems that being born to poverty carries tremendous residual, psychological, and sociological consequences even for those who have moved out of poverty.

Presumably both stress and material disadvantage are important causes of ill-health among the poor. But which is more important? And what would be the best way to address these problems? If stress is a major cause of ill-health, what interventions to alleviate it might be beneficial? On the other hand, if material disadvantage is a major cause of ill-health among the poor, then extensive changes are needed in the environment in which the poor live.

People who are not poor often casually ascribe their aches, pains and even more serious afflictions to 'stress', which is a far more serious problem for the poor. As we discussed in chapter 14 on stress management, one of the key principles is to have a sense of control. Poor people almost always have a complete lack of control over their lives as well as the way society and its institutions treat them.

In closing, I would like to make a sincere appeal to all the readers to do their bit to help the poor in our midst. The help can be in any form and it may be as simple as acknowledging that the beggars and the others living in our streets and below the flyovers are humans too and deserve to be treated with basic decency. If you can pause for a moment and think what it must be like to be treated with contempt by others, you will begin to get a sense for how the poor live every day. Empathy and even a small donation to any charitable institution working with the poor will go a long way in helping them.

Appendix 1 | The Race

To get the answer to the question of who won the race, we first need to get a little more technical and define what we mean by 'win'. If we say that a win means the first team to identify and describe the chemical structure of a hormone that directs the pituitary to release some other hormone, then the winner is the Schally team. They submitted the details of a hormone that controls the way in which the pituitary regulates the thyroid hormone. In what we could call a photo finish in scientific terms, Guillemin and his team submitted a paper reaching the same conclusion almost five weeks later.

But, several months before these papers, it was Guillemin and his team that published a paper that identified the chemical structure of the hormone that indirectly regulates the thyroid release and claimed that though they had not isolated the chemical from the brain mash, it would be present in the mash. So, in effect, they were the first to find the hormone from the brain to the pituitary but they just could not separate it out from the brain mash.

I will let the reader decide the real winner of the race. Suffice it to say that the Nobel Prize committee decided to award the prize to both the scientists in recognition of their contributions to this field.

| Appendix 2 | Introduction to the Theory of Natural Selection |

Common usage of the word 'evolution' conveys the idea that living things in our world have come into being through processes starting from a primeval mass of subatomic particles and radiation, over approximately 20 billion years.

A more precise understanding of the above statement divides the 'atoms to people' transition into four realms:

- *Cosmology* is the branch of astronomy that deals with the origin, and formation of the general structure of the universe.
- *Biogenesis* refers to first life—the production of living organisms from inanimate matter.
- *Microevolution* or *speciation* refers to population and species change through time. There are many published examples of speciation if, by the development of a new 'species', we mean the development of a new population of individuals, which will not breed, with the original population to produce fertile offspring. Microevolution

is a scientific fact, which no one, including creationists, disputes.

- *Macroevolution* or *general evolution* refers the progression to more complex forms of life. The mechanisms of macroevolution are still being researched and there is no definitive theory to explain the process.

The popular mechanisms for explaining microevolution are 'mutation' and 'natural selection'.

- *Mutations* are 'mistakes' introduced into the genetic material used for reproduction, which can occur for example as a result of exposure to radiation. Naturally occurring mutations are rare, and it is acknowledged that of those that do occur, almost all have a negative effect (in fact, some creationists argue there is not a single known case of a truly positive mutation, one having no negative side-effects). The occasional positive mutation, giving some benefit to the organism, provides the 'new material' for natural selection to operate on.
- *Natural selection* is based on the observation that there is variation among individuals in a population. Natural selection states that those individuals who possess some advantage in the environment (such as being a faster runner) are more likely to leave more offspring, thereby increasing the probability of passing the advantage on to future generations. Natural selection is what 'retains' the occasional positive mutation and causes the population to 'advance' is some way. Consider the case when

we treat a bacterial infection with an antibiotic. Among the billions of bacteria there may be some that possess resistance to the antibiotic. The process of natural selection will now result in the survival of the bacteria with the immunity and their percentage in the general population will be higher. Given sufficient time, the majority of the bacteria will have this advantageous immunity.

A classic example of natural selection that is often quoted in the literature on the subject is the peppered moth changing its predominant colour in response to environmental pollution during the industrial era of England. Here, the predominance of white moths was shifted to dark moths, allowing for camouflage against predatory birds, as the trees darkened due to industrial pollution. Before the population shift occurred, both light and dark moths were present. The environment allowed one shade to flourish. However, what if the pollution covering the trees on which they rested was a bright purple, making both the light and dark moths highly visible. Would the moths become purple? Experiments and knowledge to date demonstrate that adaptation has limits beyond which no more change is possible.

Appendix 3 | How Does the Heart Work?

The heart is divided into four chambers: (see Figure A):

- Right Atrium (RA)
- Right Ventricle (RV)
- Left Atrium (LA)
- Left Ventricle (LV)

Figure A: Chambers of the Heart

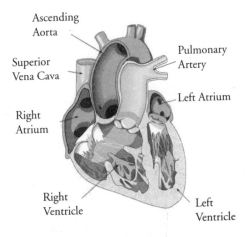

Each chamber has a sort of one-way valve at its exit that prevents blood from flowing backwards. When each chamber contracts, the valve at its exit opens. When it stops contracting, the valve closes so that blood does not flow backwards.

Tricuspid valve - is at the exit of the right atrium.
Pulmonary valve - is at the exit of the right ventricle.
Mitral valve - is at the exit of the left atrium.
Aortic valve - is at the exit of the left ventricle.

When the heart muscle contracts or beats (called systole) it pumps blood out of the heart. The heart contracts in two stages. In the first stage, the right and left atria contract at the same time, pumping blood to the right and left ventricles. Then the ventricles contract together to propel blood out of the heart. Then the heart muscle relaxes (called diastole) before the next heartbeat. This allows blood to fill up the heart again.

Index

About the Author

Vinay Joshi, an entrepreneur, is presently Chairman, MedStream Pharmaceuticals, a start-up biotechnology company that is engaged in the research, development and marketing of novel drug delivery systems. Prior to this, he founded and was president of Fincalc Publishing Corp., Boca Raton, Florida, USA.

Mr Joshi earlier co-founded Comutec Robotics Inc., Troy, New York, and served as the Company's President and director of research. He has written several research articles in the areas of 3-D graphics, robotics and mathematical modelling of fixed income securities. Vinay Joshi is also co-author of *Managing Indian Banks* (second edition), published by Response Books.